BASIC ALGEBRA FOR KIDS

A simple Step by Step Guide For Learning, Homework and Revision

Deborah Waugh

Published by Deborah Waugh Limited

ISBN-13: 978-1530448302
ISBN-10: 1530448301

♥ Dedicated to my son, Todd ♥
For whom I originally wrote this book as a
straightforward way to learn algebra and as a
handy reference book for homework and revision.

Contents

CHAPTER 1

WHAT ARE EQUATIONS

Algebra looks difficult but by understanding the basic rules **you can do it!**

So you can easily do this sum   **2 + 2 = 4**   how easy was that!

Guess what – that sum is an **equation**.

It has numbers **both sides** of an **equals sign** which gives the same number.

All these are equations too:

$$5 + 8 = 13$$

$$9 - 4 = 5$$

$$6 \times 7 = 42$$

Think of these sums as a **see saw (teeter totter)** with the equals sign as the balancing pivot ▲ both sides equal the same number and balance.

It is very important to keep this balance!

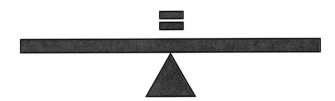

Basic rule: If you change one side – you must make the **same change** to the **other side** of the equals sign:

So   4 + **5 + 8 = 13 + 4**   **Both sides equal 17**

x 3 **9 – 4 = 5 × 3**   **Both sides equal 15**

- 5 **6 × 7 = 42 - 5**   **Both sides equal 37**

CHAPTER 2

ALGEBRA

Algebra is just sums which are equations (like those on the previous page).

Algebra sums are equations which include letters like....

x, y, n, m or any letter....

These letters are just numbers which we do not know yet.

We just need to **solve** (work out) the equations to find out what number the letter represents.

Using the sums from page 1, it is easy to see what number each letter equals.

$5 + 8 = 13$ could be $x + 8 = 13$ so $x = 5$

$9 - 4 = 5$ could be $y - 4 = 5$ so $y = 9$

$6 \times 7 = 42$ could be $m \times 7 = 42$ so $m = 6$

So now we need to look at the methods of how we work out different types of equation – **remembering both sides must always balance!**

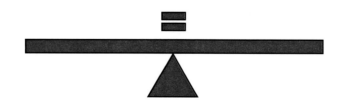

CHAPTER 3

SUBTRACTING A NUMBER
FROM BOTH SIDES OF THE EQUATION

Remember, the basic rule in algebra is:

Do the same to BOTH sides of the equal sign to keep the balance

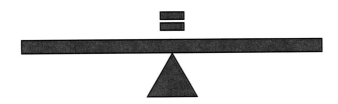

So how do we find what number x is in the equation below?

$$x + 3 = 5$$

We need to do the sum so that only x is on the left of the equal sign.

We do this by **subtracting 3 on both sides.**

$$x + 3 \boxed{-3} = 5 \boxed{-3}$$

$$x + 0 = 2$$

$$x = 2$$

CHAPTER 4

ADDING A NUMBER TO BOTH SIDES OF THE EQUATION

Remember, the basic rule in algebra is:

Do the same to BOTH sides of the equal sign to keep the balance

So how do we find what number x is in the equation below?

$$x - 4 = 6$$

We need to do the sum so that only x is on the left of the equal sign.

We do this by **adding 4 on both sides.**

$$x - 4 \boxed{+4} = 6 \boxed{+4}$$

$$x + 0 = 10$$

$$x = 10$$

CHAPTER 5

DIVIDING BOTH SIDES OF THE EQUATION BY THE SAME NUMBER

Again, the basic rule in algebra is:

Do the same to BOTH sides of the equal sign to keep the balance

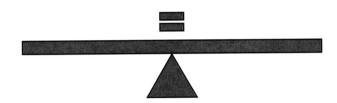

So how do we find what number x is in the equation below?

$$3x = 15$$

This time we have 3 x's on the left and we only want one x.

To get one x we must:

Divide both sides by the number of x's we have on the left - which in our example is **3**.

$$3x \div 3 = 15 \div 3$$
$$x = 5$$

CHAPTER 6

MULTIPLYING BOTH SIDES OF THE EQUATION BY THE SAME NUMBER

Again, the basic rule in algebra is:

Do the same to BOTH sides of the equal sign to keep the balance

So how do we find what number x is in the equation below?

It looks more difficult – but it's not!

$$\frac{x}{3} = 6$$

We only have 1/3 of an x on the left and we need to make it into a **whole x**.

To get a whole x we must:

Multiply both sides by the number which is the **DENOMINATOR** – which is

the number **under x** - which in our example is **3**.

$$\boxed{3 \times} \quad \frac{x}{3} = 6 \boxed{\times 3}$$

Then cancel down next – both 3's on the left cancel each out other leaving x

$$x = 6 \times 3$$

$$x = 18$$

CHAPTER 7

COMBINING CALCULATIONS
CHAPTER 3 AND CHAPTER 5

Some equations will require more than one step to get x by itself.

It looks difficult but breaking it down into steps will help you.

So how do we find what number x is in the equation below?

$$4x + 3 = 27$$

STEP 1

We need to do the sum so that only **4x** is on the left of the equal sign.

We do this by **subtracting 3 on both sides.**

$$4x + 3 \boxed{-3} = 27 \boxed{-3}$$

Which leaves us with:

$$4x = 24$$

STEP 2

Now we are left with **4x's** on the left and we only want one x.

To get one x we must **divide** both sides by the number of x's we have on the left - which in our example is **4.**

$$4x \boxed{\div 4} = 24 \boxed{\div 4}$$

$$x = 6$$

CHAPTER 8

COMBINING CALCULATIONS
CHAPTER 4 AND CHAPTER 5

Again, some equations will require more than one step to get x by itself.

This looks difficult but breaking it down into steps will help you.

So how do we find what number x is in the equation below?

$$5x - 4 = 21$$

STEP 1

We need to do the sum so that only **5x** is on the left of the equal sign.

We do this by **adding 4 on both sides.**

$$5x - 4 \boxed{+4} = 21 \boxed{+4}$$

Which leaves us with:

$$5x \qquad = 25$$

STEP 2

Now we are left with **5x**'s on the left and we only want one x.

To get one x we must **divide** both sides by the number of x's we have on the left - which in our example is **5.**

$$5x \boxed{\div 5} \qquad = 25 \boxed{\div 5}$$

$$x \qquad = 5$$

CHAPTER 9

WHEN x IS A MINUS IN THE EQUATION

So how do we find what number x is in the equation below?

$$6 - x = 2$$

STEP 1

First, we need to do the sum so that only x is on the left of the equal sign.

We do this by **subtracting 6 on both sides.**

$$6 \boxed{-6} - x = 2 \boxed{-6}$$

Leaves us with: $$-x = -4$$

STEP 2

But we need x to be **positive** not negative.

In Algebra we can change the sign from $-x$ to $+x$ but we must:

Do the same to BOTH sides of the equal sign to keep the balance

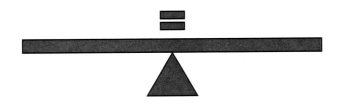

So $$x = 4$$

CHAPTER 10

MORE COMPLEX EQUATIONS
x's ON BOTH SIDES OF EQUAL SIGN

More complex equations will require more steps to get x by itself.

This looks very difficult but break it down into steps.

So how do we find what number x is in the equation below?

$$6x + 2 = 4x + 8$$

STEP 1

First we need to get the x's to the left hand side of the equal sign.

We do this by **subtracting 4x on both sides.**

$$6x \boxed{-4x} + 2 = 4x \boxed{-4x} + 8$$

Leaves us with: $2x + 2 = 8$

STEP 2

Next we need to get the numbers to the right hand side of the equal sign.

We do this by **subtracting 2 on both sides.**

$$2x + 2 \boxed{-2} = 8 \boxed{-2}$$

Leaves us with: $2x = 6$

STEP 3

Now we are left with **2x**'s on the left and we only want one x.

To get one x we must **divide** both sides by the number of x's we have on the left - which in our example is **2.**

$$2x \boxed{\div 2} = 6 \boxed{\div 2}$$

$$x = 3$$

CHAPTER 11

MORE COMPLEX EQUATIONS
x's ON BOTH SIDES OF EQUAL SIGN

More complex equations will require more than one step to get x by itself.

This looks very difficult but break it down into steps.

So how do we find what number x is in the equation below?

$$8x - 16 = 2x - 4$$

STEP 1

First we need to get the x's to the left hand side of the equal sign.

We do this by **subtracting 2x on both sides.**

$$8x \boxed{-2x} - 16 = 2x \boxed{-2x} - 4$$

Leaves us with: $6x \qquad - 16 = - 4$

STEP 2

Next we need to get the numbers to the right hand side of the equal sign.

We do this by **adding 16 on both sides.**

$$6x - 16 \boxed{+16} = - 4 \boxed{+16}$$

Leaves us with: $6x \qquad\qquad = 12$

STEP 3

Now we are left with **6x**'s on the left and we only want one x.

To get one x we must **divide** both sides by the number of x's we have on the left - which in our example is **6.**

$$6x \boxed{\div 6} \qquad = 12 \boxed{\div 6}$$

$$x \qquad\qquad = 2$$

CHAPTER 12

MORE COMPLEX EQUATIONS
x's ON BOTH SIDES OF EQUAL SIGN

More complex equations will require more than one step to get x by itself.

Just break it down into the steps as you have done in Chapter 10 and 11.

So how do we find what number x is in the equation below?

$$5x - 4 = 2x + 14$$

STEP 1

First we need to get the x's to the left hand side of the equal sign.

We do this by **subtracting $2x$ on both sides.**

$$5x \boxed{-2x} - 4 = 2x \boxed{-2x} + 14$$

Leaves us with: $3x - 4 = 14$

STEP 2

Next we need to get the numbers to the right hand side of the equal sign.

We do this by **adding 4 on both sides.**

$$3x - 4 \boxed{+4} = 14 \boxed{+4}$$

Leaves us with: $3x = 18$

STEP 3

Now we are left with **$3x$'s** on the left and we only want one x.

To get one x we must **divide** both sides by the number of x's we have on the left - which in our example is **3**.

$$3x \boxed{\div 3} = 18 \boxed{\div 3}$$

$$x = 6$$

CHAPTER 13

MORE COMPLEX EQUATIONS
x's ON BOTH SIDES OF EQUAL SIGN

Now look at a slightly different equation......

Just break it down into the steps as you have done in Chapter 10 to 12.

So how do we find what number x is in the equation below?

$$7x - 2x = 3x + 8$$

STEP 1

First we need to do the straightforward subtraction of x's on the left hand side of equal sign.

$$7x - 2x = 3x + 18$$

Leaves us with: $5x = 3x + 18$

STEP 2

Next we need to get the x's to the left hand side of the equal sign.

We do this by **subtracting 3x on both sides.**

$$5x \boxed{-3x} = 3x \boxed{-3x} + 18$$

Leaves us with: $2x = 18$

STEP 3

Now we are left with **2x's** on the left and we only want one x.

To get one x we must **divide** both sides by the number of x's we have on the left - which in our example is **2.**

$$2x \boxed{\div 2} = 18 \boxed{\div 2}$$

$$x = 9$$

CHAPTER 14

EVEN MORE COMPLEX EQUATIONS
x's BOTH SIDES OF EQUAL SIGN

So now you are getting confident you can try this ......

How do we find what number x is in the equation below?

$$3x + 4x -2 + 8 = 3x + 7 - x + 9$$

STEP 1

First we need to just work out the x's on each side of equal sign.

$$3x + 4x -2 + 8 = 3x - x + 7 + 9$$

Leaves us with: $\quad 7x \quad -2 + 8 = 2x \quad + 7 + 9$

STEP 2

Next we need to just work out the numbers on each side of equal sign.

$$7x \quad -2 + 8 = 2x \quad + 7 + 9$$

Leaves us with: $\quad 7x \quad + 6 = 2x \quad + 16$

STEP 3

Then we need to get the x's to the left hand side of the equal sign.

We do this by **subtracting $2x$ on both sides**

$$7x \boxed{-2x} + 6 = 2x \boxed{-2x} + 16$$

Leaves us with: $\quad 5x \quad + 6 = 16$

Now we need to get the numbers to the right hand side of the equal sign.

We do this by **subtracting 6 on both sides.**

$$5x + 6 \boxed{-6} = 16 \boxed{-6}$$

Leaves us with: $5x \qquad = 10$

STEP 5

Finally we are left with **5x**'s on the left and we only want one x.

To get one x we must **divide** both sides by the number of x's we have on the left - which in our example is **5.**

$$5x \boxed{\div 5} \quad = 10 \boxed{\div 5}$$

$$x \qquad\quad = 2$$

CHAPTER 15

EQUATIONS WITH BRACKETS

Equations can also contain brackets so follow the steps below ......

So how do we find what number x is in the equation below?

$$4 + 2 (x + 1) = 22$$

STEP 1

First we need to **work out** the bracket (**expand** the bracket).

You need to multiply the number outside the bracket with both items inside the bracket so.

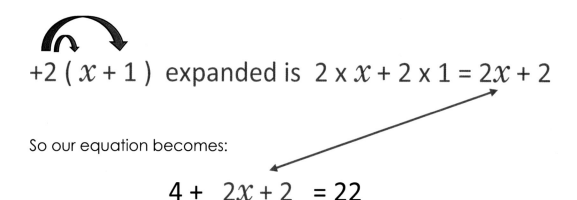

+2 (x + 1) expanded is $2 \times x + 2 \times 1 = 2x + 2$

So our equation becomes:

$$4 + 2x + 2 = 22$$

STEP 2

Next we need to just work out the numbers on left hand side of equal sign.

$$4 + 2x + 2 = 22$$

Leaves us with: $2x + 6 = 22$

<u>STEP 3</u>

Now we need to get the numbers to the right hand side of the equal sign.

We do this by **subtracting 6 on both sides.**

$$2x + 6 \boxed{-6} = 22 \boxed{-6}$$

Leaves us with: $\quad 2x \qquad\qquad = 16$

<u>STEP 4</u>

Finally we are left with **2x**'s on the left and we only want one **x**.

To get one **x** we must **divide** both sides by the number of **x**'s we have on the left - which in our example is **2.**

$$2x \boxed{\div 2} \quad = 16 \boxed{\div 2}$$

$$x \qquad\qquad = 8$$

CHAPTER 16

EQUATIONS WITH MORE BRACKETS

Use the same method from Chapter 15 for equations with more brackets – and follow the steps below ......

So how do we find what number x is in the equation below?

$$9 (2x - 2) + 2 (3x + 5) = 2 (10x + 8)$$

STEP 1

First we need to **work out each** bracket (**expand** each bracket).

You need to multiply the number outside each bracket with both items inside the bracket so do one at a time.

$+9 (2x - 2)$ expanded is $+9 \times 2x$ $+9 \times -2 = 18x - 18$

So our equation becomes:

$$18x - 18 + 2 (3x + 5) = 2 (10x + 8)$$

STEP 2

Next bracket

$+2 (3x + 5)$ expanded is $+2 \times 3x$ $+2 \times 5 = 6x + 10$

So our equation becomes:

$$18x - 18 + 6x + 10 = 2 (10x + 8)$$

Next bracket

+2 (10x + 8) expanded is +2 x 10x +2 x 8 = 20x +16

So our equation becomes:

$$18x - 18 + 6x + 10 = 20x + 16$$

STEP 4

Then we need to just work out the x's on each side of equal sign.

$$18x - 18 + 6x + 10 = 20x + 16$$

Leaves us with: $24x$ $- 18 + 10 = 20x + 16$

STEP 5

Next we need to just work out the numbers on each side of equal sign.

$$24x \quad -18 + 10 = 20x + 16$$

Leaves us with: $24x$ $- 8$ $= 20x + 16$

STEP 6

Then we need to get the x's to the left hand side of the equal sign.

We do this by **subtracting 20x on both sides.**

$$24x \boxed{-20x} - 8 = 20 x \boxed{-20x} + 16$$

Leaves us with: $4x$ $- 8$ $=$ 16

Now we need to get the numbers to the right hand side of the equal sign.

We do this by **adding 8 on both sides.**

$$4x - 8 \boxed{+8} = 16 \boxed{+8}$$

Leaves us with: $4x \qquad = 24$

STEP 8

Finally we are left with **4x**'s on the left and we only want one x.

To get one x we must **divide** both sides by the number of x's we have on the left - which in our example is **4.**

$$4x \boxed{\div 4} \quad = 24 \boxed{\div 4}$$

$$x \qquad = 6$$

CHAPTER 17

SUBSTITUTION

Substitution is where you are given an equation and a value for the letter in the equation. You just need to substitute the number for the letter in the equation.

EXAMPLE

If $x = 2$ find the value of $5x + 4$

So we substitute x with **2** in the equation giving us:

$$5 \times 2 + 4 \quad \text{which equals}$$

$$= 10 + 4 = 14$$

EXAMPLE

If $y = 3$ find the value of $30 - 2y^2$

So we substitute y with **3** in the equation giving us:

$$= 30 - 2 \times 3^2 \quad \text{which equals}$$

$$= 30 - 2 \times 9$$

$$= 30 - 18 = 12$$

SUBSTITUTION - Continued

EXAMPLE

If $p = 4$ find the value of

$$\frac{3p - 8}{5(p - 1)}$$

Substituting p with **4** becomes:

$$\frac{3 \times 4 - 8}{5(4 - 1)}$$

Next week need to expand the bracket on the bottom:

$$\frac{3 \times 4 - 8}{5(4 - 1)}$$

Now we are left with:

$$\frac{12 - 8}{20 - 5} = \frac{4}{15}$$

CHAPTER 18

INDICES

Indices are where there is a small number or letter showing at the top right hand of a number or letter.

Like 5^3 which is just another way of showing **5 x 5 x 5**

> This is also called **5 to the power of 3** or **5 cubed.**

or x^2 which is just x **x** x

> This is also called x **to the power of 2** or x **squared**.

These small numbers are called **indices** and there are special rules for multiplication and division of indices, and also where there are brackets.

MULTIPLICATION

Where you have a common number (same number) multiplied with indices you must **ADD** the indices.

Numbers	Algebra
$3^6 \times 3^3 = 3^{6+3} = 3^9$	$x^a \times x^b = x^{a+b}$

DIVISION

Where you have a common number (same number) divided with indices you must **SUBTRACT** the indices

Numbers	Algebra
$3^6 \div 3^3 = 3^{6-3} = 3^3$	$x^a \div x^b = x^{a-b}$

Division of indices can also be shown as:

$$\frac{3^6}{3^3}$$

$$\frac{x^a}{x^b}$$

SPECIAL RULE: Any number or letter to the **power of zero always equals 1**

$$3^0 = 1$$

$$x^0 = 1$$

INDICES - Continued

<u>BRACKETS</u>

Where there are indices inside and outside of brackets, you **MULTIPLY** the indices.

<u>Numbers</u>   <u>Algebra</u>

$$(3^6)^3 \ = \ 3^{6 \times 3} \ = \ 3^{18} \qquad\qquad (x^a)^b \ = \ x^{a \times b}$$

<u>MIXED NUMBERS AND LETTERS</u>

Now let's look at more algebra indices where there are more than just one number or letter.

The **rule** here is always **work out the numbers first** then work out the letters.

Example: $(3x^3)^2 \ = \ 3^2 \ x^{3 \times 2} \ = \ 9\, x^6$

Example: $3x^2 \ \times \ 10x^3 \ = \ 3 \times 10 \ x^{2+3} \ = \ 30\, x^5$

Example: $20x^7 \ \div \ 4x^2 \ = \ 20 \div 4 \ x^{7-2} \ = \ 5\, x^5$

Example: $(2x^3 y^2)^4 \ = \ 2^4 \ x^{3 \times 4} \ y^{2 \times 4} \ = \ 16\, x^{12}\, y^8$

In this example the **4** outside the bracket must be multiplied by each Index number inside the bracket. **Note** that **2** is same as **2^1**

CHAPTER 19

FACTORISING - SINGLE BRACKETS

Factorising in algebra means collecting (pulling out) the common (same) number or letter which appears in each part of an equation.

You just need to follow the steps:

Look at this example $\qquad$ $xy + 3x$ $\qquad$ x is the common term

So the equation becomes $x(y + 3)$

This is the reverse of multiplying brackets which we looked at in chapter 15.

It's that simple – so let's look at some more difficult ones:

<u>EXAMPLE</u>

$$9x^2 + x \qquad x \text{ is the common term}$$

So the equation becomes $x(9x + 1)$

<u>EXAMPLE</u>

$$30t^4 - 6t^3$$

In this example we have **2** common terms **6** and t^3

So the equation becomes $6t^3(5t - 1)$

CHAPTER 20

QUADRATIC EQUATIONS - EXPANDING BRACKETS

Now we will look at quadratic equations where brackets need to be multiplied.

You just need to follow the steps:

$$(x + 3) \; (x + 2)$$

<u>STEP 1</u>

Multiply both items on the left hand side of each bracket.

$$x \times x = x^2$$

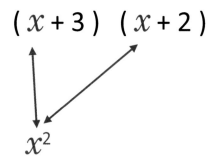

Put this on the left hand side of your answer.

<u>STEP 2</u>

Multiply both items on the right hand side of each bracket.

$$3 \times 2 = 6$$

$$(x + 3) \; (x + 2)$$

$$+ 6$$

Put this on the right hand side of your answer.

Multiply inner 2 items of each bracket.

$$3 \times x = 3x$$

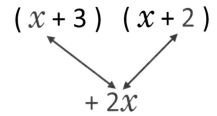

$$+ 3x$$

Put this on the left hand inner side of your answer.

Multiply outer 2 items of each bracket.

$$x \times 2 = 2x$$

$$(x + 3) \quad (x + 2)$$

$$+ 2x$$

Put this on the right hand inner side of your answer.

ANSWER

Finally, we just need to simplify the **x**'s in the middle.

So far we have:

$$x^2 + 3x + 2x + 6$$

Which becomes:

$$x^2 \quad + 5x \quad + 6$$

SUMMARY

Overall summary of the above steps:

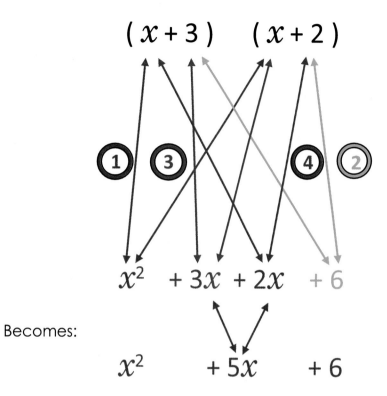

$$(x + 3) \quad (x + 2)$$

$$x^2 \ + 3x \ + 2x \ + 6$$

Becomes:

$$x^2 \qquad + 5x \qquad + 6$$

CHAPTER 21

QUADRATIC EQUATIONS - EXPANDING BRACKETS

Now we will look at a different equation with a minus sign in one of the brackets.

You just need to follow the steps shown in Chapter 20:

$$(4x - 3) \ (x + 5)$$

<u>STEP 1</u>

Multiply both items on the left hand side of each bracket.

$$4x \times x = 4x^2$$

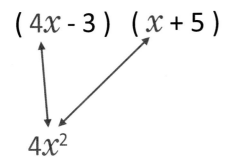

Put this on the left hand side of your answer.

<u>STEP 2</u>

Multiply both items on the right hand side of each bracket.

$$- 3 \times 5 = - 15$$

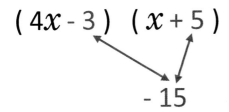

Put this on the right hand side of your answer.

Multiply inner 2 items of each bracket.

$$-3 \times x = -3x$$

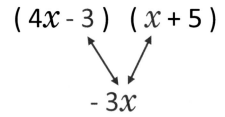

Put this on the left hand inner side of your answer.

Multiply outer 2 items of each bracket.

$$4x \times 5 = 20x$$

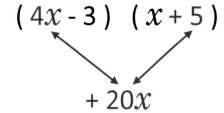

Put this on the right hand inner side of your answer.

<u>ANSWER</u>

Finally, we just need to simplify the x's in the middle.

So far we have:

$$4x^2 - 3x + 20x - 15$$

Becomes:

$$4x^2 + 17x - 15$$

CHAPTER 22

QUADRATIC EQUATIONS - EXPANDING BRACKETS

This equation is one to be aware of so you know how to do it correctly.
Again, you just need to follow the steps shown in Chapter 20:

$$(x + 3)^2$$

First, think of this as if the bracket was a number like 3^2 which is simply

$$3 \times 3$$

So it is important to write our equation in full before doing the steps below.

Now it becomes: $(x + 3) \; (x + 3)$

STEP 1

Multiply both items on the left hand side of each bracket.

$$x \times x = x^2$$

$$(x + 3) \; (x + 3)$$

$$x^2$$

Put this on the left hand side of your answer.

STEP 2

Multiply both items on the right hand side of each bracket.

$$3 \times 3 = 9$$

$$(x + 3) \; (x + 3)$$

$$+ 9$$

Put this on the right hand side of your answer.

Multiply inner 2 items of each bracket.

$$3 \times x = 3x$$

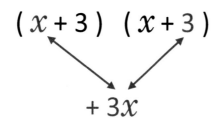

$$(x + 3) \ (x + 3)$$

$$+ 3x$$

Put this on the left hand inner side of your answer.

Multiply outer 2 items of each bracket.

$$x \times 3 = 3x$$

$$(x + 3) \ (x + 3)$$

$$+ 3x$$

Put this on the right hand inner side of your answer.

<u>ANSWER</u>

Finally, we just need to simplify the x's in the middle.

So far we have:

$$x^2 + 3x + 3x + 9$$

Becomes:

$$x^2 \quad + 6x \quad + 9$$

CHAPTER 23

QUADRATIC EQUATIONS - EXPANDING BRACKETS

In this example there is a number outside the brackets.

So how do we work this out?

$$2\,(\,3x + 1\,)\,\,(\,2x + 5\,)$$

STEP 1

The easiest way is to expand the number and the left hand bracket first as a separate equation, then do the normal double bracket expansion.

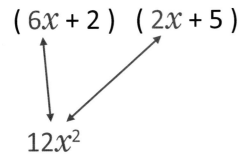

$$2\,(\,3x + 1\,)\,\,(\,2x + 5\,)$$

So we get:

$$(\,6x + 2\,)\,\,(\,2x + 5\,)$$

STEP 2

Multiply both items on the left hand side of each bracket.

$$6x \,\times\, 2x \,=\, 12x^2$$

$$(\,6x + 2\,)\,\,(\,2x + 5\,)$$

$$12x^2$$

Put this on the left hand side of your answer.

Multiply both items on the right hand side of each bracket.

$$2 \text{ x } 5 = 10$$

$$(6x + 2) \quad (2x + 5)$$

$$+10$$

Put this on the right hand side of your answer.

Multiply inner 2 items of each bracket.

$$2 \text{ x } 2x = 4x$$

$$(6x + 2) \quad (2x + 5)$$

$$+ 4x$$

Put this on the left hand inner side of your answer.

Multiply outer 2 items of each bracket.

$$6x \text{ x } 5 = 30x$$

$$(6x + 2) \quad (2x + 5)$$

$$+ 30x$$

Put this on the right hand inner side of your answer.

Finally, we just need to simplify the x's in the middle.

So far we have:

$$12x^2 + 4x + 30x + 10$$

Becomes:

$$12x^2 \qquad + 34x \qquad + 10 \; \bigstar$$

You may be asking why not expand the double brackets first and then multiply by the number outside the brackets? That is a really good question – you can do it this way and still get exactly the same answer. It just a question of preference on how to do the question. Let's have a look doing it that way:

STEP 1

Expand the brackets first, leaving the answer inside brackets with the number kept outside the brackets.

$$2\,(\,3x + 1\,)\,(\,2x + 5\,)$$

STEP 2

Multiply both items on the left hand side of each bracket.

$$3x \times 2x = 6x^2$$

$$(\,3x + 1\,)\,(\,2x + 5\,)$$

$$6x^2$$

Put this on the left hand side of your answer.

Multiply both items on the right hand side of each bracket.

$$1 \times 5 = 5$$

$$(3x + 1) \quad (2x + 5)$$

$$+5$$

Put this on the right hand side of your answer.

Multiply inner 2 items of each bracket.

$$1 \times 2x = 2x$$

$$(3x + 1) \quad (2x + 5)$$

$$+ 2x$$

Put this on the left hand inner side of your answer.

Multiply outer 2 items of each bracket.

$$3x \times 5 = 15x$$

$$(3x + 1) \quad (2x + 5)$$

$$+ 15x$$

Put this on the right hand inner side of your answer

Next put the equation back together and in brackets but first simplify the x's in the middle.

REMEMBER we still have the number outside the brackets:

So far we have:

$$2 \ (6x^2 + 2x + 15x + 5)$$

Becomes:

$$2 \ (6x^2 \quad + 17x \ + 5)$$

STEP 7

Finally, we just need to multiply 2 with each item in the brackets:

$$2 \ (6x^2 \quad + 17x \ + 5)$$

Expanding the brackets the answer is:

$$12x^2 \quad + 34x \ + 10 \ \bigstar$$

CHAPTER 24

QUADRATIC EQUATIONS - EXPANDING BRACKETS

<u>ADDITION - TWO SETS OF DOUBLE BRACKETS</u>

Now we will look at how to work out the addition of 2 sets of double brackets.

You just need to follow the steps shown in Chapter 20:

$$(x + 7) (x - 3) + (x - 5) (x - 4)$$

<u>STEP 1</u>

First expand the brackets on the left of the plus sign.

Multiply both items on the left hand side of each bracket.

$$x \times x = x^2$$

$$(x + 7) \quad (x - 3)$$

$$x^2$$

Put this on the left hand side of your answer.

<u>STEP 2</u>

Multiply both items on the right hand side of each bracket.

$$7 \times -3 = -21$$

$$(x + 7) \quad (x - 3)$$

$$-21$$

Put this on the right hand side of your answer.

Multiply inner 2 items of each bracket.

$$7 \times x = 7x$$

$$(x + 7) \ (x - 3)$$

$$7x$$

Put this on the left hand inner side of your answer.

STEP 4

Multiply outer 2 items of each bracket.

$$x \times -3 = -3x$$

$$(x + 7) \ (x - 3)$$

$$-3x$$

Put this on the right hand inner side of your answer.

STEP 5

Put the left hand equation together and simplify the x's in the middle.

So far we have:

$$x^2 + 7x - 3x - 21$$

Becomes:

$$x^2 + 4x - 21$$

Now look at the brackets on the right of the plus sign – if there is no number outside the brackets it is important to get into the habit of putting a 1 on the outside. Why? You will understand why when you follow the steps below – especially when there is a subtraction – see next Chapter.

Our equation so far is:

$$x^2 + 4x - 21 \boxed{+\ 1}\,(\,x - 5\,)\,(\,x - 4\,)$$

Now expand the brackets on the right of the plus sign leaving the 1 for now.

Multiply both items on the left hand side of each bracket.

$$x \times x = x^2$$

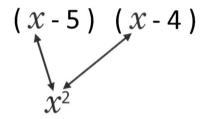

Put this on the left hand side of your answer.

STEP 7

Multiply both items on the right hand side of each bracket.

$$-\ 5 \times -\ 4 = +\ 20$$

$$(\,x - 5\,)\ (\,x - 4\,)$$

$$+20$$

Put this on the right hand side of your answer.

Multiply inner 2 items of each bracket.

$$- 5 \times x = -5x$$

$$(x - 5) \; (x - 4)$$

$$-5x$$

Put this on the left hand inner side of your answer.

Multiply outer 2 items of each bracket.

$$x \times -4 = -4x$$

$$(x - 5) \; (x - 4)$$

$$-4x$$

Put this on the right hand inner side of your answer.

Put the right hand equation together and simplify the x's in the middle.

So far we have:

$$x^2 - 5x - 4x + 20$$

Becomes:

$$(x^2 - 9x + 20)$$ <u>NOTE</u>: Keep this in brackets

Our equation so far is now:

$$x^2 + 4x - 21 \boxed{+1} (x^2 - 9x + 20)$$

The final step is to multiply the **+1** outside the bracket on the right by each item inside the bracket.

$$x^2 + 4x - 21 \boxed{+1} (x^2 - 9x + 20)$$

Which leaves:

$$x^2 + 4x - 21 + x^2 - 9x + 20$$

As you can see – because this was an addition the signs on the right hand side do not change.

STEP 12

Now we need to add the x^2's and put on the left hand side of the equation.

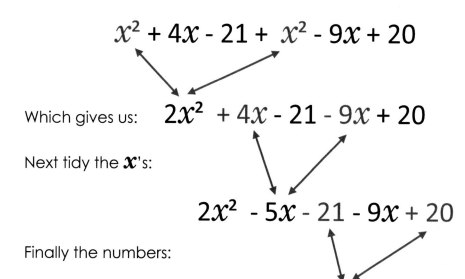

$$x^2 + 4x - 21 + x^2 - 9x + 20$$

Which gives us: $\quad 2x^2 + 4x - 21 - 9x + 20$

Next tidy the x's:

$$2x^2 - 5x - 21 - 9x + 20$$

Finally the numbers:

Answer: $\quad 2x^2 - 5x - 1$

CHAPTER 25

QUADRATIC EQUATIONS - EXPANDING BRACKETS

SUBTRACTION - TWO SETS OF DOUBLE BRACKETS

Now we will look at how to work out the addition of 2 sets of double brackets.

You just need to follow the steps shown in Chapter 20:

$$(x + 4) (x - 2) - (x - 3) (x + 7)$$

STEP 1

First expand the brackets on the left of the minus sign.

Multiply both items on the left hand side of each bracket.

$$x \times x = x^2$$

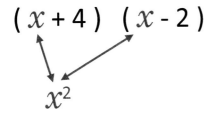

Put this on the left hand side of your answer.

STEP 2

Multiply both items on the right hand side of each bracket.

$$4 \times -2 = -8$$

$$(x + 4) (x - 2)$$

$$-8$$

Put this on the right hand side of your answer.

Multiply inner 2 items of each bracket.

$$4 \times x = 4x$$

$$(x + 4) (x - 2)$$

$$4x$$

Put this on the left hand inner side of your answer.

STEP 4

Multiply outer 2 items of each bracket.

$$x \times -2 = -2x$$

$$(x + 4) (x - 2)$$

$$-2x$$

Put this on the right hand inner side of your answer.

STEP 5

Put the left hand equation together and simplify the x's in the middle.

So far we have:

$$x^2 + 4x - 2x - 8$$

Becomes:

$$x^2 + 2x - 8$$

Now look at the brackets on the right of the plus sign – if there is no number outside the brackets- remember it is important to get into the habit of putting
a 1 on the outside.

Our equation so far is:

$$x^2 + 2x \ - 8 \ \boxed{- 1} (x - 3) (x + 7)$$

Now expand the brackets on the right of the plus sign leaving the 1 for now.

Multiply both items on the left hand side of each bracket.

$$x \times x = x^2$$

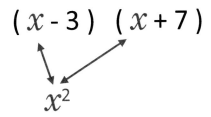

Put this on the left hand side of your answer.

STEP 7

Multiply both items on the right hand side of each bracket.

$$- 3 \times 7 = -21$$

$$(x - 3) (x + 7)$$

$$-21$$

Put this on the right hand side of your answer.

Multiply inner 2 items of each bracket.

$$-3 \times x = -3x$$

$$(x-3)(x+7)$$

$$-3x$$

Put this on the left hand inner side of your answer.

STEP 9

Multiply outer 2 items of each bracket.

$$x \times 7 = 7x$$

$$(x-3)(x+7)$$

$$7x$$

Put this on the right hand inner side of your answer.

STEP 10

Put the right hand equation together and simplify the x's in the middle.

So far we have:

$$x^2 - 3x + 7x - 21$$

Becomes:

$$(x^2 + 4x - 21)$$ <u>NOTE</u>: Keep this in brackets

Our equation so far is now:

$$x^2 + 2x - 8 \boxed{-1}(x^2 + 4x - 21)$$

The final step is to multiply the **-1** outside the bracket on the right by each item inside the bracket.

$$x^2 + 2x - 8 \boxed{-1}(x^2 + 4x - 21)$$

Which leaves:

$$x^2 + 2x - 8 - x^2 - 4x + 21$$

IMPORTANT – because the number outside the bracket (**-1**) was a minus – the sign for each item inside the bracket has now changed.

STEP 12

Now we need to tidy the x^2's which as you see $x^2 - x^2 = 0$ so they are removed.

$$x^2 + 2x - 8 - x^2 - 4x + 21$$

Which gives us: $\quad 2x - 8 - 4x + 21$

Next tidy the X's:

$$-2x - 8 + 21$$

Finally the numbers:

Answer: $\quad -2x + 13$

CHAPTER 26

FACTORISING QUADRATIC EQUATIONS

In Chapters 20 to 25 we covered quadratic equations where we had to multiply the brackets to get our answer.

Factorising quadratic equations is just doing the reverse – taking the equation and getting back to the 2 brackets.

Remember this from Chapter 20:

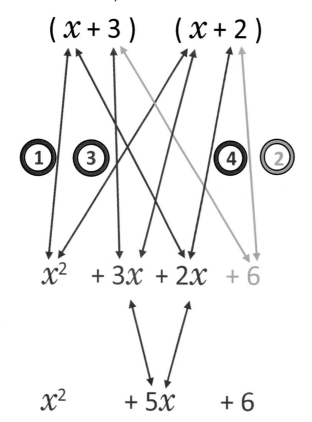

$$(x + 3) \quad (x + 2)$$

$$x^2 \quad + 3x \quad + 2x \quad + 6$$

Becomes:

$$x^2 \quad + 5x \quad + 6$$

In the following example we need to work back to get to the brackets:

$$x^2 \quad + 8x \quad + 15$$

$$x^2 \qquad + 8x \qquad + 15$$

<u>STEP 1</u>

We already know that $\quad x \times x = x^2$

The left hand side of each bracket must be $\quad x$

So far we have $\qquad (x \,?\,?) \; (x \,?\,?)$

<u>STEP 2</u>

The 2 numbers on the right hand side of each bracket multiplied together = 15

The only 2 sets of numbers that multiply together to get 15 are
1 x 15 and 3 x 5.

Given that the middle number is **8x** and 3 plus 5 = 8 we can work on the numbers on the right hand side of each bracket being 3 and 5.

So now we have $\qquad (x \,?\, 3) \; (x \,?\, 5)$

<u>STEP 3 and STEP 4</u>

We need to get to **8x** in the middle, so we need to consider whether each bracket contains a plus or a minus.

Multiply inner 2 items of each bracket.

$$3 \times x = 3x$$

$$(x \,?\, 3) \; (x \,?\, 5)$$

$$?\, 3x$$

Multiply outer 2 items of each bracket.

$$x \times 5 = 5x$$

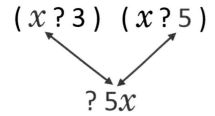

$$(x\,?\,3)\quad (x\,?\,5)$$

$$?\,5x$$

To get **8x** both brackets must contain + plus signs.

So our answer is: $\quad (x + 3)\quad (x + 5)$

SUMMARY

Overall summary of the above steps:

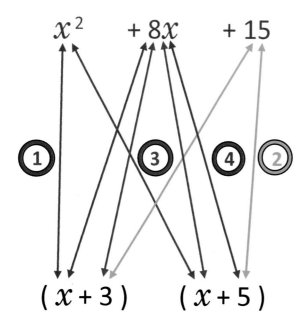

CHAPTER 27

FACTORISING QUADRATIC EQUATIONS

This equation is one that has a simple rule to remember.

$$x^2 \quad - \ 12x \quad + \ 20$$

RULE:
Where the equation has a minus sign in the middle and a plus at the end –
BOTH BRACKETS will contain MINUS signs.

STEP 1

We already know that $\quad x \times x \ = \ x^2$

The left hand side of each bracket must be x

So far we have $\quad (x - ?) \ (x - ?)$

STEP 2

The 2 numbers on the right hand side of each bracket multiplied together = 20

There are 3 sets of numbers that multiply together to get 20 which are
1 x 20, 2 x 10 and 4 x 5.

Given that the middle number is **12x** and 2 plus 10 = 12 we can work on the numbers on the right hand side of each bracket being 2 and 10. We also know from the rule above that both brackets contain minus signs.

So now we have $\quad (x - 2) \ (x - 10)$

We just need to check that we get **-12x** in the middle
Multiply inner 2 items of each bracket.

$$-2 \times x = -2x$$

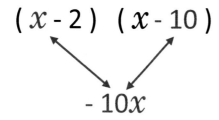

$$(x - 2) \ (x - 10)$$

$$- 2x$$

Multiply outer 2 items of each bracket.

$$x \times -10 = -10x$$

$$(x - 2) \ (x - 10)$$

$$- 10x$$

So our answer is: $\quad (x - 2) \ (x - 10)$

SUMMARY

Overall summary of the above steps:

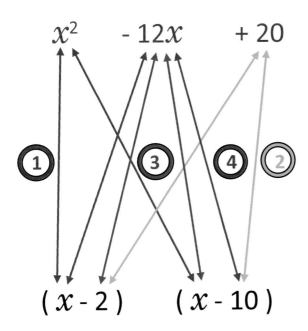

CHAPTER 28

FACTORISING QUADRATIC EQUATIONS

This equation is unusual as there are no x's in the middle.

$$x^2 \quad - 4$$

It is important to follow the steps as before to work out the brackets.

STEP 1

We already know that $\quad x \times x = x^2$

The left hand side of each bracket must be x

So far we have $\quad (x \; ? \, ?) \; (x \; ? \, ?)$

STEP 2

The 2 numbers on the right hand side of each bracket multiplied together = 4

There are 2 sets of numbers that multiply together to get 4 which are
1 x 4, 2 x 2.

Given that there is no middle x number and 2 minus 2 = 0 we can work on the numbers on the right hand side of each bracket being 2 and 2 with one being a plus sign and the other being a minus sign.

So now we have $\quad (x + 2) \; (x - 2)$

STEP 3 and STEP 4

We just need to check that we get no x's in the middle
Multiply inner 2 items of each bracket.

$$2 \times x = 2x$$

$$(x+2) \quad (x-2)$$

$$+2x$$

Multiply outer 2 items of each bracket.

$$x \times -2 = -2x$$

$$(x-2) \quad (X-2)$$

$$-2x$$

So our answer is: $(x+2) \quad (x-2)$

<u>SUMMARY</u>

Overall summary of the above steps:

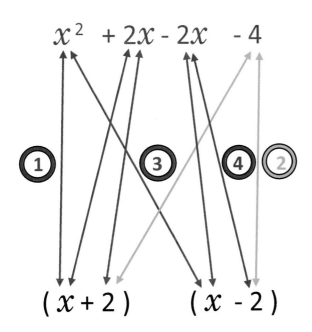

$$x^2 + 2x - 2x - 4$$

(1)   (3)   (4) (2)

$(x+2) \quad (x-2)$

CHAPTER 29

EQUATIONS WITH FRACTIONS - ALGEBRAIC FRACTIONS

Equations with fractions are also known as **Algebraic Fractions.**

These questions look really difficult – but don't panic – first you need to know which type of question you are being asked and then follow the step by step method to get to the answer.

Types of algebraic fraction question:

1. <u>SIMPLIFY</u>   Chapter 30

   When you are asked to **SIMPLIFY** the fraction equation – this means put the fraction equation question into its **simplest reduced form**. It is really important to check **first** to see if the top or the bottom of the fraction needs to be **factorised** and then you need to see if the fraction can be cancelled down (reduced).
   So remember – **Simplify** = **Factorise?** then **Cancel down**.

2. <u>ADDITION</u>   Chapters 32 to 33

   Where you need to **add** algebraic fractions you treat them exactly the same as if it were normal **number fractions – the same rules apply**.

3. <u>SUBTRACTION</u>   Chapter 34

   Where you need to **subtract** algebraic fractions you treat them exactly the same as if it were normal **number fractions – the same rules apply**.

4. <u>MULTIPLICATION</u>   Chapter 35

   Where you need to **multiply** algebraic fractions you treat them exactly the same as if it were normal **number fractions – the same rules apply**.

5. <u>DIVISION</u>   Chapter 36

   Where you need to **divide** algebraic fractions you treat them exactly the same as if it were normal **number fractions – the same rules apply**

6. SOLVE   Chapters 37 to 42

Where you are asked to **SOLVE** the fraction equation – it means **find the value of x**. When solving algebraic fraction equations - first you need to change them into an equation without fractions by clearing (removing) the denominators. This is called the Clearing of Fractions and you will see how to do this in chapter 37.

Now we will look at all 5 of these different kinds of algebraic fraction question in separate chapters so you can follow the steps and you will understand how to do these.

CHAPTER 30

ALGEBRAIC FRACTIONS - SIMPLIFY

The clue is in the question as it will start with **SIMPLIFY** the fraction equation.

All this means is that you need to put the fraction equation into it's **simplest reduced form.**

FIRST you will need to check if the top or the bottom of the fraction needs to be **factorised** (pull out the common items – Chapter 19)
THEN you need to see if the fraction can be cancelled down (reduced).

<u>Example</u>

Simplify $$\frac{4x+8}{2}$$

<u>STEP 1</u>

Can the top be factorised?   Yes – 4 is a common item and can be pulled out.

Can the bottom be factorised? **No**

So we get: $$\frac{4(x+2)}{2}$$

<u>STEP 2</u>

Can the fraction be cancelled down? Yes it can - the 4 at the top and the 2 at the bottom can be cancelled down:

$$\frac{\cancel{4}^{\,2}\,(x+2)}{\cancel{2}^{\,1}}$$

Leaving us with: $$2\,(x+2)$$

So let's now look at a more difficult example:

<u>Example</u>

Simplify $\dfrac{x^2 - 4}{(x+2)}$

<u>STEP 1</u>

Can the top be factorised?   Yes it can - if you go back to chapters 26 - 28 to remind yourself on the steps of how on to factorise quadratics.

Can the bottom be factorised? No

So we get: $\dfrac{(x+2)\,(x-2)}{(x+2)}$

<u>STEP 2</u>

Can the fraction be cancelled down? Yes it can – there is $(x+2)$ at the top and the bottom that can be cancelled down:

$$\dfrac{\cancel{(x+2)}(x-2)}{\cancel{(x+2)}}$$

Leaving us with: $(x - 2)$

CHAPTER 31

ALGEBRAIC FRACTIONS – ADDITION & SUBTRACTION RULES

When simplifying algebraic fractions – you apply exactly the same rules that you use for addition, subtraction, multiplication and division of normal number fractions.

It is important at this stage to remind ourselves of the **3 rules for denominators** in **addition and subtraction** of fractions.

1. ## SAME DENOMINATORS

Addition and subtraction of fractions is very straightforward where the denominators are the same.

	Normal fraction		Algebraic fraction
Simplify:	$\dfrac{1}{6} + \dfrac{4}{6}$		$\dfrac{1}{x} + \dfrac{4}{x}$

The **common denominator stays the same** and just the top items are added.

$$= \frac{1+4}{6} \qquad\qquad = \frac{1+4}{x}$$

$$= \frac{5}{6} \qquad\qquad = \frac{5}{x}$$

Just remember to do a **final check** to see if your final answer can be cancelled down at the end.

ALGEBRAIC FRACTIONS - ADDITION & SUBTRACTION RULES
Continued

2. <u>DIFFERENT DENOMINATORS WITH COMMON ITEMS (FACTORS)</u>

Where the denominators are different you must first look to see if there are any common numbers or letters – as you need to **make the denominators the same.**

<u>Normal fraction</u>   <u>Algebraic fraction</u>

Simplify: $\dfrac{1}{3} + \dfrac{5}{6}$ $\dfrac{1}{x} + \dfrac{5}{6x}$

The lowest common denominator   The lowest common denominator

is 6 - as 3 and 6 divide into 6.   is $6x$ – as x and $6x$ divide into $6x$.

So to get a common denominator that is the same for both fractions, we must multiply the **top and bottom** of **one** of the fractions by the **same number**. The fraction is still in the same proportion (equivalent fraction) – you have just **SUPERSIZED** it!

<u>Normal fraction</u>   <u>Algebraic fraction</u>

$$X6 \nearrow\!\!\!\searrow \dfrac{1}{3} + \dfrac{5}{6} \qquad\qquad X6 \nearrow\!\!\!\searrow \dfrac{1}{x} + \dfrac{5}{6x}$$

$$= \dfrac{6}{6} + \dfrac{5}{6} \qquad\qquad\qquad = \dfrac{6}{6x} + \dfrac{5}{6x}$$

$$= \dfrac{6+5}{6} \qquad\qquad\qquad\quad = \dfrac{6+5}{6x}$$

$$= \dfrac{11}{6} \qquad\qquad\qquad\quad\; = \dfrac{11}{6x}$$

Just remember to do a **final check** to see if your final answer can be cancelled down at the end.

ALGEBRAIC FRACTIONS - ADDITION & SUBTRACTION RULES
Continued

3. DIFFERENT DENOMINATORS WITH COMMON ITEMS (FACTORS) Continued

But we can also get fractions where the denominators with common numbers or letters need **both** fractions changing to get a common denominator for each fraction.

<table>
<tr><td></td><td>Normal fraction</td><td>Algebraic fraction</td></tr>
<tr><td>**Simplify:**</td><td>$\dfrac{1}{6} + \dfrac{3}{4}$</td><td>$\dfrac{1}{6x} + \dfrac{3}{4x}$</td></tr>
</table>

The lowest common denominator here is 12 - as 6 and 4 divide into 12.

The lowest common denominator here is 12x – as 6x and 4x divide into 12x.

To get a common denominator **both** fractions need to be changed. We must multiply the **top and bottom** of **both** fractions by the number which gives us denominators that are the same. The fractions are still in the same proportion (equivalent fractions) – you have just **SUPERSIZED** them!

<table>
<tr><td>Normal fraction</td><td>Algebraic fraction</td></tr>
<tr><td>X 2 $\dfrac{1}{6} + \dfrac{3}{4}$ X 3</td><td>X 2 $\dfrac{1}{6x} + \dfrac{3}{4x}$ X 3</td></tr>
<tr><td>= $\dfrac{2}{12} + \dfrac{9}{12}$</td><td>= $\dfrac{2}{12x} + \dfrac{9}{12x}$</td></tr>
<tr><td>= $\dfrac{2+9}{12}$</td><td>= $\dfrac{2+9}{12x}$</td></tr>
<tr><td>= $\dfrac{11}{12}$</td><td>= $\dfrac{11}{12x}$</td></tr>
</table>

Just remember to do a **final check** to see if your final answer can be cancelled down at the end.

ALGEBRAIC FRACTIONS - ADDITION & SUBTRACTION RULES
Continued

4. <u>DIFFERENT DENOMINATORS WITH NO COMMON ITEMS (FACTORS)</u>

As in the previous examples - where the denominators are different you must first look to see if there are any common numbers or letters – as you need to make the denominators the same.

Sometimes there are no common numbers or items other than multiplying the bottom denominators together to get a common denominator.

Remember whatever you multiply the bottom fraction by – you must also multiply the top by the same number.

Normal fraction	Algebraic fraction
Simplify: $\dfrac{1}{6} + \dfrac{3}{7}$	$\dfrac{1}{6x} + \dfrac{3}{7x}$

Here we need to multiply 6 x 7 to get a common denominator of 42

Here we need to multiply 6 x 7 to a common denominator of 42x

So to get a common denominator **both** fractions need to be changed. We must multiply the **top and bottom** of **both** fractions by the number which gives us denominators that are the same. The fractions are still in the same proportion (equivalent fractions) – you have just **SUPERSIZED** them!

Normal fraction	Algebraic fraction
X 7 $\dfrac{1}{6}$ + $\dfrac{3}{7}$ X 6	X 7 $\dfrac{1}{6x}$ + $\dfrac{3}{7x}$ X 6
= $\dfrac{7}{42} + \dfrac{18}{42}$	= $\dfrac{7}{42x} + \dfrac{18}{42x}$
= $\dfrac{7 + 18}{42}$	= $\dfrac{7 + 18}{42x}$
= $\dfrac{25}{42}$	= $\dfrac{25}{42x}$ ★

Just remember to do a **final check** to see if your final answer can be cancelled down at the end.

Before we leave this example – you may be asking why the denominator was $42x$ why did we not just use $6x$ times $7x = 42x^2$?

Well the answer is you can, but if you do this there is one **extra** final cancel down step at the end which is crucial to remember.

So the above example would become:

<table>
<tr><td>Normal fraction</td><td>Algebraic fraction</td></tr>
<tr><td>**Simplify:** $\dfrac{1}{6} + \dfrac{3}{7}$</td><td>$\dfrac{1}{6x} + \dfrac{3}{7x}$</td></tr>
</table>

Here we need to multiply 6 x 7 to get a common denominator of 42

Here we need to multiply $6x$ x $7x$ to get a common denominator of $42x^2$

Normal fraction

$$X\,7 \nearrow \dfrac{1}{6} + \dfrac{3}{7} \nwarrow X\,6$$

$$= \dfrac{7}{42} + \dfrac{18}{42}$$

$$= \dfrac{7 + 18}{42}$$

$$= \dfrac{25}{42}$$

Algebraic fraction

$$X\,7x \nearrow \dfrac{1}{6x} + \dfrac{3}{7x} \nwarrow X\,6x$$

$$= \dfrac{7x}{42x^2} + \dfrac{18x}{42x^2}$$

$$= \dfrac{7x + 18x}{42x^2}$$

$$= \dfrac{25\cancel{x}}{42x^{\cancel{2}}}$$

EXTRA STEP

As you can see there is x on top and x^2 on the bottom which cancels down to take out the x on the top and x^2 on the bottom cancels to $42x$.

Just remember to do a **final check** to see if the numbers can be cancelled down too.

Giving the same final answer as above: $= \dfrac{25}{42x}$ ★

64

CHAPTER 32

ALGEBRAIC FRACTIONS - ADDITION

You apply exactly the same rules that you use for addition of normal number fractions as in number 2 in chapter 31.

ADDITION   Normal fraction   Algebraic fraction

Simplify: $\dfrac{3}{8} + \dfrac{3}{12}$ $\dfrac{3}{8x} + \dfrac{3}{12x}$

The lowest common denominator here is   The lowest common denominator here is

24 - as 8 and 12 divide into 24 $24x$ – as $8x$ and $12x$ divide into $24x$

Normal   = **24** ← LOWEST COMMON DENOMINATOR → Algebraic = **24x**

Now, whatever number you need to multiply the bottom by to get the lowest common denominator – you must multiply the top by the same number:

X 3 $\dfrac{3}{8}$ + $\dfrac{3}{12}$ X 2   X 3 $\dfrac{3}{8x}$ + $\dfrac{3}{12x}$ X 2

= $\dfrac{9}{24} + \dfrac{6}{24}$ = $\dfrac{9}{24x} + \dfrac{6}{24x}$

= $\dfrac{9+6}{24}$ = $\dfrac{9+6}{24x}$

= $\dfrac{15}{24}$ = $\dfrac{15}{24x}$

Now cancel down where possible:

= ÷ 3 $\dfrac{15}{24}$ = ÷ 3 $\dfrac{15}{24x}$

= $\dfrac{5}{8}$ = $\dfrac{5}{8x}$

CHAPTER 33

ALGEBRAIC FRACTIONS - ADDITION – MORE COMPLEX

You apply exactly the same rules that you use for addition of normal number fractions as in number 3 in chapter 31.

Simplify:
$$\frac{2}{(x+1)} + \frac{1}{(x+2)}$$

In more complex algebraic fractions we can only multiply the bottom denominators together to get a common denominator. So the common denominator here is

$$(x+1)\,(x+2)$$

Now, whatever you need to multiply the bottom by to get the common denominator – you must multiply the top by exactly the same:

$$= \quad x\,(x+2)\; \frac{2}{(x+1)} + \frac{1}{(x+2)}\; x\,(x+1)$$

$$= \quad \frac{2(x+2)}{(x+1)(x+2)} + \frac{1(x+1)}{(x+1)(x+2)}$$

$$= \quad \frac{2(x+2)+1(x+1)}{(x+1)(x+2)}$$

Next we need to expand the brackets on the top – chapter 15.

$$= \quad \frac{2x+4+x+1}{(x+1)(x+2)}$$

Now simplify the top:
$$\frac{2x+4+x+1}{(x+1)(x+2)}$$

$$= \quad \frac{3x+5}{(x+1)(x+2)}$$

CHAPTER 34

ALGEBRAIC FRACTIONS - SUBTRACTION

You apply exactly the same rules that you use for subtraction of normal number fractions as in number 2 in chapter 31.

SUBTRACTION:

Normal fraction	Algebraic fraction
Simplify: $\dfrac{3}{8} - \dfrac{3}{12}$	$\dfrac{3}{8x} - \dfrac{3}{12x}$

The lowest common denominator here is 24 - as 8 and 12 divide into 24.

The lowest common denominator here is $24x$ – as $8x$ and $12x$ divide into $24x$

Normal $= 24 \leftarrow$ LOWEST COMMON DENOMINATOR $\rightarrow$ Algebraic $= 24x$

Now, whatever number you need to multiply the bottom by to get the lowest common denominator – you must multiply the top by the same number:

$$\text{X}3 \diagup\!\!\!\searrow \dfrac{3}{8} - \dfrac{3}{12} \searrow\!\!\!\diagup \text{X}2 \qquad \text{X}3 \diagup\!\!\!\searrow \dfrac{3}{8x} - \dfrac{3}{12x} \searrow\!\!\!\diagup \text{X}2$$

$$= \dfrac{9}{24} - \dfrac{6}{24} \qquad\qquad = \dfrac{9}{24x} - \dfrac{6}{24x}$$

$$= \dfrac{9-6}{24} \qquad\qquad = \dfrac{9-6}{24x}$$

$$= \dfrac{3}{24} \qquad\qquad = \dfrac{3}{24x}$$

Now cancel down where possible:

$$= \div 3 \diagup\!\!\!\searrow \dfrac{3}{24} \qquad\qquad = \div 3 \diagup\!\!\!\searrow \dfrac{3}{24x}$$

$$= \dfrac{1}{8} \qquad\qquad\qquad = \dfrac{1}{8x}$$

CHAPTER 35

ALGEBRAIC FRACTIONS - MULTIPLICATION

MULTIPLICATION:

Normal fraction	Algebraic fraction
Simplify: $\dfrac{2}{15} \times \dfrac{9}{10}$	$\dfrac{(y-5)}{(y+1)} \times \dfrac{(y+1)}{(y+2)}$

Normal rule for multiplication of fractions – first see if you can **cancel down**:

$$\overset{1}{\cancel{2}}_{} \times \overset{3}{\cancel{9}}_{}$$
$$\underset{5}{\cancel{15}} \qquad \underset{5}{\cancel{10}}$$

$$\frac{(y-5)}{\cancel{(y+1)}} \times \frac{\cancel{(y+1)}}{(y+2)}$$

Now simply multiply the top and the bottom:

$$= \quad \frac{3}{25} \qquad\qquad\qquad = \quad \frac{(y-5)}{(y+2)}$$

CHAPTER 36

ALGEBRAIC FRACTIONS - DIVISION

DIVISION:

Normal fraction	Algebraic fraction

Simplify: $\dfrac{6}{7} \div \dfrac{3}{7}$ $\dfrac{(y-5)}{(y+1)} \div \dfrac{(y+2)}{(y+1)}$

Normal rule for division of fractions – **FLIP** the second fraction then treat as a

MULTIPLICATION – cancel down then multiply the top and bottom.

$=$ $\dfrac{6}{7} \times \dfrac{7}{3}$ $=$ $\dfrac{(y-5)}{(y+1)} \times \dfrac{(y+1)}{(y+2)}$

Now see if you can cancel down:

$$\overset{2}{\underset{1}{\cancel{6}}} \times \overset{1}{\underset{1}{\cancel{7}}}$$
$$\dfrac{\cancel{6}}{\cancel{7}} \times \dfrac{\cancel{7}}{\cancel{3}}$$

$\dfrac{(y-5)}{\cancel{(y+1)}} \times \dfrac{\cancel{(y+1)}}{(y+2)}$

Now simply multiply the top and the bottom:

$=$ $\dfrac{2}{1} = 2$ $=$ $\dfrac{(y-5)}{(y+2)}$

CHAPTER 37

SOLVING ALGEBRAIC FRACTIONS

Solve: $\dfrac{x}{3} + 2 = 6$

In order to **SOLVE** (find the value for x) for an equation with fractions –

you must change it into an equation WITHOUT FRACTIONS.

This is called the **CLEARING OF FRACTIONS**.

<u>STEP 1</u>

First, we need to do the sum so that only $\dfrac{x}{3}$ is on the left of the equal sign.

We do this by **subtracting 2 on both sides.**

$$\dfrac{x}{3} + 2 \boxed{-2} = 6 \boxed{-2}$$

$$\dfrac{x}{3} = 4$$

<u>STEP 2</u>

Now we only have $\dfrac{1}{3}$ of an x on the left and we need to make it into a **whole x**

To get a whole x and remove the denominator (Clearing of Fractions) we must **multiply**

both sides by the number which is the **DENOMINATOR** – this is the number **under x** -

which in our example is **3.**

$$\boxed{3 \times} \dfrac{x}{3} = 4 \boxed{\times 3}$$

Then cancel down next – both 3's on the left cancel each other out leaving x

$$x = 4 \times 3$$

$$x = 12$$

SOLVING ALGEBRAIC FRACTIONS - Continued

Solve: $\dfrac{x}{5} - 3 = 2$

STEP 1

First, we need to do the sum so that only $\dfrac{x}{5}$ is on the left of the equal sign.

We do this by **adding 3 on both sides.**

$$\dfrac{x}{5} - 3 \boxed{+3} = 2 \boxed{+3}$$

$$\dfrac{x}{5} = 5$$

STEP 2

We only have $\dfrac{1}{5}$ of an x on the left and we need to make it into a **whole x.**

To get a whole x and remove the denominator (Clearing of Fractions) we must **multiply** both sides by the number which is the **DENOMINATOR** – this is the number **under x** - which in our example is **5.**

$$\boxed{5 \times} \dfrac{x}{5} = 5 \boxed{\times 5}$$

Then cancel down next – both 5's on the left cancel each other leaving x

$$x = 5 \times 5$$

$$x = 25$$

CHAPTER 38

SOLVING MORE COMPLEX ALGEBRAIC FRACTIONS

In Chapter 29 we looked at simple equations with fractions and you may want to have a quick look back at that chapter.

Solving algebraic fractions looks very difficult but it's not!

You just need to know the method then you can tackle them with ease.

So how do we find x in this equation:

Solve: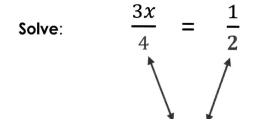

$$\frac{3x}{4} = \frac{1}{2}$$

STEP 1

Where we have fractions, the **denominators** (numbers at the bottom of each fraction) need removing first. Remember this is called **Clearing of Fractions**.

We do this by **multiplying each side of the equal sign by the lowest number** that **both** denominators - bottom numbers - can divide into. And if you are not sure what number to use you can simply use the bottom numbers multiplied by each other.

IMPORTANT NOTE: In Chapters 29 to 36 where we were **SIMPLIFYING** fractions we multiplied the top and the bottom of the fraction to get the denominators to be the same – this was just making it a bigger equivalent fraction. Now we are **SOLVING** fractions so in order to **remove** the denominators (Clear the Fractions) we multiply **THE TOP ONLY** by the lowest number and then cancel down.

In our example above, we have 4 and 2 so start off with 4 x 2 = 8. Is this the lowest number we can use – no it is 4 because 4 can be divided by 4 and 2.

But note that using 4 or 8 that you will **still get the same answer** – it's just that using the lowest number makes the cancelling down easier.

So we need to **multiply both sides by 4.**

$$\frac{\cancel{4}}{1} \quad \times \quad \frac{3x}{\cancel{4}} \quad = \quad \frac{1}{\cancel{2}} \quad \times \quad \frac{\cancel{4}^{\,2}}{1}$$

Now cancel down (see red arrows above) – both 4's on the left cancel each other out leaving 3x.

On the right we have 4 divided by 2 leaving 2 at the top.

So our equation is now:

$$3x \quad = 2$$

STEP 3

Now we are left with **3x**'s on the left and we only want one x.

To get one x we must **divide** both sides by the number of x's we have on the left - which in our example is **3.**

$$3x \boxed{\div 3} \quad = 2 \boxed{\div 3}$$

$$x \quad = \quad \frac{2}{3}$$

CHAPTER 39

SOLVING MORE COMPLEX ALGEBRAIC FRACTIONS
Continued

Solve: $$\frac{x}{2} = \frac{1}{6} + \frac{x}{3}$$

<u>STEP 1</u>

Again, the **denominators** (numbers at the bottom of each fraction) need removing.

We do this by **multiplying the TOP of every item on each side of the equal sign by the lowest number** that all the 3 bottom numbers can divide into.

In our example we have 2, 3 and 6. The number is 6 because it can be divided by 2, 3 and 6.

So we need to **multiply all items on both sides by 6.**

$$\frac{\overset{3}{\cancel{6}}}{1} \times \frac{x}{\cancel{2}} = \frac{\cancel{6}}{1} \times \frac{1}{\cancel{6}} + \frac{\overset{2}{\cancel{6}}}{1} \times \frac{x}{\cancel{3}}$$

<u>STEP 2</u>

Now cancel down (see red arrows above) – on the left of the equal sign 6 divided by 2 is 3 so you are left with 3x.

On the right the two 6's cancel to 1 and to the right of the plus sign 6 divided by 3 is 2 so we are left with 2x at the top.

So our equation is now:

$$3x = 1 + 2x$$

<u>STEP 3</u>

Next we need to get the x's to the left hand side of the equal sign.

We do this by **subtracting 2x on both sides.**

$$3x \boxed{-2x} = 1 + 2x \boxed{-2x}$$

Leaves us with: $$x = 1$$

CHAPTER 40

SOLVING MORE COMPLEX ALGEBRAIC FRACTIONS
Continued

Solve: $$\frac{x-3}{2} = \frac{x-2}{3}$$

<u>STEP 1</u>

As before, the **denominators** (numbers at the bottom of each fraction) need removing.

We do this by **multiplying the TOP of each side of the equal sign by the lowest number** that all the bottom numbers can divide into.

In our example we have 2 and 3 so start off with 2 x 3 = 6. Is this the lowest number we can use – yes it is.

So we need to **multiply each item on both sides by 6.**

<u>STEP 2</u>

Now cancel down (see red arrows above) – on the left of the equal sign you are left with

$3(x-3)$

On the right of the equal sign we are left with $2(x-2)$

So our equation is now:

$$3(x-3) \ = 2(x-2)$$

We now have brackets to work out both sides of the equal sign.

STEP 3

First we need to **work out** the brackets (**expand** the brackets) on the left

Remember: You need to multiply the number outside the bracket with both   items inside the bracket so

$3(x-3)$ expanded is $3 \times x + 3 \times -3 = 3x - 9$

STEP 4

Next bracket on the right side.

$2(x-2)$ expanded is $2 \times x + 2 \times -2 = 2x - 4$

So our equation becomes:

$$3x - 9 = 2x - 4$$

STEP 5

Now we need to get the x's to the left hand side of the equal sign.

We do this by **subtracting $2x$ on both sides**

$$3x \boxed{-2x} - 9 = 2x \boxed{-2x} - 4$$

Leaves us with: $x - 9 = -4$

STEP 6

Finally, we need to get the numbers to the right hand side of the equal sign.

We do this by **adding 9 on both sides.**

$$x - 9 \boxed{+9} = -4 \boxed{+9}$$

Leaves us with: $x = 5$

76

CHAPTER 41

SOLVING MORE COMPLEX ALGEBRAIC FRACTIONS
Continued

Solve:
$$\frac{28}{x-1} = \frac{8}{x+4}$$

<u>STEP 1</u>

This time we have x's at the bottom instead of numbers – the method to remove the denominators is exactly the same.

We do this by **multiplying the TOP of each side of the equal sign by the denominators multiplied by each other** and then cancelling down.

In our example we have x **-1** and x **+4** so multiplied by each other we get

$$(x \text{ -1}) (x \text{ +4})$$

There is no need to expand the brackets!

So now we **multiply both sides of the equal sign by (x -1) (x +4)**

$$\frac{(x-1)\,(x+4)}{1} \times \frac{28}{x-1} = \frac{8}{x+4} \times \frac{(x-1)\,(x+4)}{1}$$

<u>STEP 2</u>

Now cancel down (see red arrows above) – on the left of the equal sign x **-1** cancels down and you are left with **28(x +4)**

On the right of the equal sign x **+4** cancels down and you are left with **8(x -1)**

So our equation is now:

$$28(x \text{ +4}) = 8(x \text{ - 1})$$

We now have brackets to work out both sides of the equal sign.

First, we need to **work out** the brackets (**expand** the brackets) on the left

Remember: You need to multiply the number outside the bracket with both   items inside the bracket so

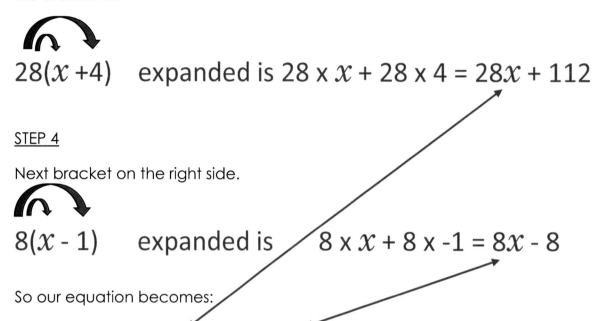

$28(x + 4)$ expanded is $28 \times x + 28 \times 4 = 28x + 112$

STEP 4

Next bracket on the right side.

$8(x - 1)$ expanded is $8 \times x + 8 \times -1 = 8x - 8$

So our equation becomes:

$$28x + 112 = 8x - 8$$

STEP 5

Now we need to get the x's to the left hand side of the equal sign.

We do this by **subtracting $8x$ on both sides**

$$28x \boxed{-8x} + 112 = 8x \boxed{-8x} - 8$$

Leaves us with: $20x + 112 = -8$

Finally, we need to get the numbers to the right hand side of the equal sign.

We do this by **subtracting 112 on both sides.**

$$20x + 112 \boxed{-112} = -8 \boxed{-112}$$

Leaves us with: $\qquad 20x \qquad = -120$

STEP 7

Finally we are left with **20x**'s on the left and we only want one x.

To get one x we must **divide** both sides by the number of x's we have on the left - which in our example is **20.**

$$20x \boxed{\div 20} = -120 \boxed{\div 20}$$

$$x \qquad = -6$$

CHAPTER 42

SOLVING MORE COMPLEX ALGEBRAIC FRACTIONS
Continued

Solve: $$\frac{4x}{x+5} - \frac{1}{x+1} = 4$$

<u>STEP 1</u>

Again, we have **x**'s at the bottom instead of numbers – the method to remove the denominators is exactly the same.

We do this by **multiplying the TOP of every item on both sides of the equal sign by the denominators multiplied by each other** and then cancelling down.

To make the calculation easier – write 4 as 4 over 1 so all are fractions.

In our example we have **x+5, x+1 and 1** so multiplied by each other we get

(x+5) (x+1)

There is no need to expand the brackets!

Now we **multiply both sides of the equal sign by (x +5) (x +1)**

$$\frac{(x+5)(x+1)}{1} \times \frac{4x}{x+5} - \frac{1}{x+1} \times \frac{(x+5)(x+1)}{1} = \frac{4}{1} \times \frac{(x+5)(x+1)}{1}$$

<u>STEP 2</u>

Now cancel down (see red arrows above) – on the left of the minus sign **x+5** cancels down and you are left with **4x(x +1)**.

On the right of the minus sign **x+1** cancels down and you are left with **1(x +5)**.
On the right of the equals sign you can drops the 1's and go back to whole numbers leaving **4(x+5)(x+1)**.

So our equation is now:

$$4x\,(x+1)\ -1(x+5)\ =\ 4(x+5)(\,x+1)$$

We now have brackets to work out both sides of the equal sign.

First we need to **work out** the brackets (**expand** the brackets) on the left

Remember: You need to multiply the number outside the bracket with both   items inside the bracket so

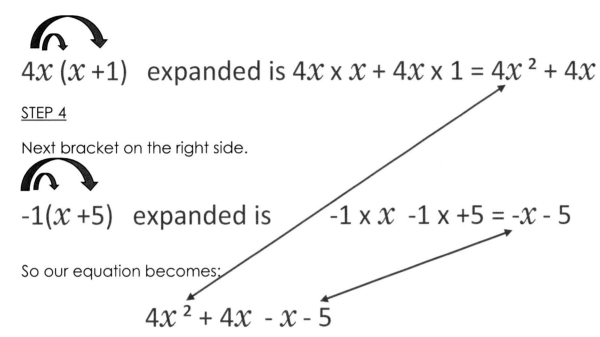

$4x\,(x+1)$ expanded is $4x \times x + 4x \times 1 = 4x^2 + 4x$

STEP 4

Next bracket on the right side.

$-1(x+5)$ expanded is $-1 \times x\; -1 \times +5 = -x - 5$

So our equation becomes:

$$4x^2 + 4x - x - 5$$

STEP 5

Now we need to work out the right hand side of the equals sign in 2 stages.

$4(x+5)(x+1)$

First, we need to multiply the brackets together – remember the steps in Chapter 20.

$$(x+5)(x+1)$$

$$= x^2 + 6x + 5$$

Finally, we need to multiply this by 4

$$4\,(x^2 + 6x + 5)$$

$$= 4x^2 + 24x + 20$$

Putting steps 3, 4 and 5 together our equation now becomes:

$$4x^2 + 4x - x - 5 = 4x^2 + 24x + 20$$

Now we need to get the x^2's to the left hand side of the equal sign.

We do this by **subtracting $4x^2$ on both sides**

$$4x^2 \boxed{-4x^2} + 4x - x - 5 = 4x^2 \boxed{-4x^2} + 24x + 20$$

You can see that the x^2 have been completely removed from both sides.

Which gives us: $4x - x - 5 = 24x + 20$

Just tidying up the left hand side **$4x - x = 3x$**

Leaves us with: $3x - 5 = 24x + 20$

In this example the most x's are on the right of the equal sign so we need to get the x's to the right hand side of the equal sign – this just makes it easier.

We do this by **subtracting $3x$ on both sides**

$$3x \boxed{-3x} - 5 = 24x \boxed{-3x} + 20$$

Leaves us with: $-5 = 21x + 20$

<u>STEP 8</u>

Now we need to get the numbers to the left hand side of the equal sign.

We do this by **subtracting 20 on both sides.**

$$- 5 \boxed{-20} = 21x + 20 \boxed{-20}$$

Which gives us: $- 25 = 21x$

But we have the x's on the right of the equal sign and we want them on the left.

We simply just flip this over like a pancake to get:

$$21x = - 25$$

<u>STEP 9</u>

Finally we are left with **21x**'s on the left and we only want one x.

To get one x we must **divide** both sides by the number of x's we have on the left - which in our example is **21.**

$$21x \boxed{\div 21} = - 25 \boxed{\div 21}$$

Leaves us with: $x = - \dfrac{25}{21}$

CHAPTER 43

SIMULTANEOUS EQUATIONS - ELIMINATION SUBTRACTION

Simultaneous equations are where you have 2 equations and the values for x and y are the same in both equations.

So look at these 2 equations:

$$2x + y = 8$$
$$x + y = 5$$

These simultaneous equations have unknowns x and y and each letter will have the same value in each equation.

So how do we work this out (**solve** this)?

<u>STEP 1</u>

First we need to eliminate either x or y by either adding or subtracting the equations.

By looking at the 2 equations we can see that by subtracting the equations we can simply eliminate y

$$2x + y = 8$$
$$\underline{x + y = 5} \ -$$

Leaves us with: $\qquad x \qquad = 3$

Now we can put the value for x into (**substitute**) either of the equations to get to the value for y. And to prove that it does not matter which of the equations you do this with we will do it with both equations so you can see.

$$2x + y = 8$$

From step 1 we know that $x = 3$ so we put it into (substitute it) the equation above.

$$2 \times 3 + y = 8$$

Gives us:
$$6 + y = 8$$

STEP 3

Next we need to get the numbers to the right hand side of the equal sign.
We do this by **subtracting 6 on both sides.**

$$6\boxed{-6} + y = 8\boxed{-6}$$

Leaves us with:
$$y = 2 \quad ★$$

STEP 4

Now we will do the same with the other equation to show the answer is the same.

$$x + y = 5$$

From step 1 we know that $x = 3$ so we put it into (substitute it) the equation above.

Gives us:
$$3 + y = 5$$

STEP 5

Next we need to get the numbers to the right hand side of the equal sign.

We do this by **subtracting 3 on both sides.**

$$3\boxed{-3} + y = 5\boxed{-3}$$

Leaves us with:
$$y = 2 \quad ★$$

CHAPTER 44

SIMULTANEOUS EQUATIONS - ELIMINATION ADDITION

Remember, simultaneous equations are where you have 2 equations and the values for x and y are the same in both equations.

So look at these 2 equations:

$$5x - 2y = 4$$

$$3x + 2y = 12$$

These simultaneous equations have unknowns x and y and each letter will have the same value in each equation.

This time we have + and – in the equation – so how do we work this out (**solve** this)?

STEP 1

First we need to eliminate either x or y by either adding or subtracting the equations.

By looking at the 2 equations we can see that by adding the equations we can simply eliminate y

$$5x - 2y = 4$$

$$\underline{3x + 2y = 12} \quad +$$

Leaves us with: $\quad 8x \qquad = 16$

Now we are left with **8x**'s on the left and we only want one **x**.

To get one **x** we must **divide** both sides by the number of **x**'s we have on the left - which in our example is **8.**

$$8x \boxed{\div 8} \quad = 16 \boxed{\div 8}$$

$$x \qquad\quad = 2$$

STEP 3

Now we can put the value for **x** into (**substitute**) either of the equations to get to the value for **y**.

Remember that it does not matter which of the equations you do this with as the answer will always be the same.

IMPORTANT TIP: Always substitute into the equation with the **+** to avoid careless errors with signs.

So we will use one of the equations we had at the start of the chapter:

$$3x + 2y = 12$$

From step 1 we know that **x = 2** so we put it into (substitute it) the equation above.

$$3 \times 2 + 2y = 12$$

Gives us:
$$6 + 2y = 12$$

STEP 4

Next we need to get the numbers to the right hand side of the equal sign.

We do this by **subtracting 6 on both sides.**

$$6 \boxed{-6} + 2y = 12 \boxed{-6}$$

Leaves us with:
$$y = 2$$

CHAPTER 45

SIMULTANEOUS EQUATIONS MORE COMPLEX ELIMINATION

In the previous 2 chapters we looked at simple elimination by adding or subtracting the equations. But what do we do when it is not straightforward?

So look at these 2 equations:

$$3x + 4y = 25$$

$$x + 2y = 11$$

This time cannot simply add or subtract the equations. We need to change one of the equations first - then we can add or subtract as before.

STEP 1

By looking at the 2 equations we can see that in order to eliminate y we need to multiply the bottom equation throughout by 2 (double it).

$$x \boxed{x2} + 2y \boxed{x2} = 11 \boxed{x2}$$

Gives us:

$$2x + 4y = 22$$

We now use this equation for the elimination:

$$3x + 4y = 25$$

$$\underline{2x + 4y = 22} -$$

Leaves us with:

$$x = 3$$

Now we can put the value for x into (**substitute**) either of the equations to get to the

value for y.

Remember that it does not matter which of the equations you do this with as the answer will always be the same.

So we will use the equation:

$$3x + 4y = 25$$

From step 1 we know that $x = 3$ so we put it into (substitute it) the equation above.

$$3 \times 3 + 4y = 25$$

Gives us: $$9 + 4y = 25$$

STEP 3

Next we need to get the numbers to the right hand side of the equal sign.

We do this by **subtracting 9 on both sides.**

$$9 \boxed{-9} + 4y = 25 \boxed{-9}$$

Leaves us with: $$y = 16$$

CHAPTER 46

SIMULTANEOUS EQUATIONS MORE COMPLEX ELIMINATION

Now we will look at what do we do when it is not straightforward one of the equations contains a negative sign.

So look at these 2 equations:

$$6x + y = 20$$

$$4x - 3y = 6$$

Again, we cannot simply add or subtract the equations. We need to change one of the equations first - then we can add or subtract as before.

STEP 1

By looking at the 2 equations we can see that in order to eliminate y we need to multiply the top equation throughout by 3 (treble it)

$$6x \boxed{\text{x3}} + y \boxed{\text{x3}} = 20 \boxed{\text{x3}}$$

Gives us: $18x + 3y = 60$

We now use this equation for the elimination:

$$18x + 3y = 60$$

$$\underline{4x - 3y = 6} +$$

Leaves us with: $22x = 66$

Now we are left with **22 x**'s on the left and we only want one x.

To get one x we must **divide** both sides by the number of x's we have on the left - which in our example is **22.**

$$22x \boxed{\div 22} \quad = 66 \boxed{\div 22}$$

$$x \quad\quad\quad = 3$$

STEP 3

Now we can put the value for x into (**substitute**) either of the equations to get to the value for y.

Remember that it does not matter which of the equations you do this with as the answer will always be the same.

IMPORTANT TIP: Always substitute into the equation with the **+** to avoid careless errors with minus signs.

So we will use the equation:

$$18x + 3y = 60$$

From step 2 we know that $x = 3$ so we put it into (substitute it) the equation above.

$$18 \times 3 + 3y = 60$$

Gives us: $\quad\quad\quad 54 + 3y = 60$

STEP 4

Next we need to get the numbers to the right hand side of the equal sign.

We do this by **subtracting 54 on both sides.**

$$54 \boxed{-54} + 3y = 60 \boxed{-54}$$

Leaves us with:
$$3y = 6$$

STEP 5

Finally, we are left with **3y**'s on the left and we only want one y.

To get one y we must **divide** both sides by the number of y's we have on the left - which in our example is **3.**

$$3y \boxed{\div 3} = 6 \boxed{\div 3}$$
$$y = 2$$

NOTE

Sometimes **both** equations may need changing (multiplying by different numbers) before you can eliminate x or y.

For example:

$$2x + 5y = 16 \quad \text{multiply by 3}$$

$$3x - 2y = 5 \quad \text{multiply by 2}$$

CHAPTER 3   Subtracting a number from both sides of the equation

1. $x + 1 = 6$

2. $x + 6 = 8$

3. $x + 4 = 10$

4. $y + 3 = 9$

5. $y + 5 = 15$

6. $n + 7 = 14$

7. $q + 9 = 13$

8. $a + 8 = 9$

9. $b + 2 = 5$

10. $z + 11 = 21$

CHAPTER 4   Adding a number to both sides of the equation

1. $x - 7 = 5$

2. $x - 2 = 4$

3. $x - 9 = 1$

4. $y - 1 = 6$

5. $y - 8 = 12$

6. $n - 4 = 2$

7. $q - 5 = 3$

8. $a - 3 = 9$

9. $b - 6 = 7$

10. $z - 13 = 8$

CHAPTER 5   Dividing both side of the equation by the same number

1. $4x = 16$

2. $8x = 56$

3. $5x = 45$

4. $6x = 66$

5. $3x = 21$

6. $7x = 56$

7. $2x = 24$

8. $9x = 81$

9. $12x = 144$

10. $15x = 90$

CHAPTER 6   Multiplying both sides of the equation by the same number

1. $\dfrac{x}{2} = 16$

2. $\dfrac{x}{3} = 8$

3. $\dfrac{x}{6} = 9$

4. $\dfrac{x}{8} = 4$

5. $\dfrac{x}{7} = 12$

6. $\dfrac{x}{4} = 6$

7. $\dfrac{x}{9} = 11$

8. $\dfrac{x}{8} = 9$

9. $\dfrac{x}{12} = 8$

10. $\dfrac{x}{5} = 7$

CHAPTER 7   Combining Calculations – Chapter 3 and Chapter 5

1. $4x + 7 = 27$

2. $2x + 8 = 16$

3. $6x + 4 = 40$

4. $5x + 6 = 51$

5. $9x + 5 = 68$

6. $3x + 9 = 36$

7. $7x + 5 = 33$

8. $12x + 3 = 111$

9. $8x + 11 = 99$

10. $15x + 12 = 72$

CHAPTER 8   Combining Calculations – Chapter 4 and Chapter 5

1. $4x - 4 = 12$

2. $2x - 5 = 55$

3. $7x - 3 = 32$

4. $2x - 22 = 22$

5. $8x - 6 = 66$

6. $5x - 8 = 47$

7. $9x - 7 = 101$

8. $6x - 5 = 43$

9. $3x - 4 = 71$

10. $12x - 9 = 135$

CHAPTER 9   When x is a minus in the equation

1. $5 - x = 1$

2. $9 - x = 6$

3. $10 - x = 8$

4. $8 - x = 5$

5. $4 - x = 3$

6. $6 - x = 2$

7. $3 - x = 1$

8. $7 - x = 4$

9. $12 - x = 7$

10. $15 - x = 9$

CHAPTER 10   More complex equations – x's on both sides of the equals sign

1. $6x + 3 = 3x + 9$

2. $2x + 5 = x + 10$

3. $9x + 2 = 2x + 44$

4. $5x + 4 = x + 48$

5. $8x + 6 = 5x + 18$

6. $4x + 7 = 2x + 55$

7. $12x + 9 = 6x + 81$

8. $7x + 8 = 4x + 35$

9. $15x + 12 = 7x + 76$

10. $3x + 11 = x + 37$

CHAPTER 11   More complex equations – x's on both sides of the equals sign

1. $4x - 7 = 3x - 4$

2. $6x - 6 = 2x - 2$

3. $9x - 13 = 7x - 5$

4. $5x - 27 = 2x - 6$

5. $7x - 16 = 5x - 8$

6. $8x - 38 = 3x - 8$

7. $13x - 117 = x - 9$

8. $10x - 87 = 3x - 3$

9. $12x - 89 = 3x - 8$

10. $15x - 72 = 4x - 6$

CHAPTER 12   More complex equations – x's on both sides of the equals sign

1. $4x - 5 = 3x + 8$

2. $5x - 1 = 2x + 11$

3. $9x - 32 = 2x + 3$

4. $2x - 9 = x + 7$

5. $8x - 5 = 4x + 43$

6. $7x - 15 = 2x + 40$

7. $6x - 8 = 3x + 19$

8. $17x - 9 = 2x + 51$

9. $14x - 7 = 5x + 101$

10. $15x - 4 = 3x + 68$

CHAPTER 13   More complex equations – x's on both sides of the equals sign

1. $9x - 2x = 3x + 8$

2. $8x - 3x = x + 12$

3. $12x - x = 2x + 63$

4. $11x - 4x = 3x + 24$

5. $5x - x = x + 9$

6. $6x + 4x = x + 72$

7. $7x + 8x = 3x + 144$

8. $3x + 14x = 2x + 75$

9. $2x + 22x = 16x + 56$

10. $4x + 9x = 2x + 132$

CHAPTER 14   Even more complex equations x's on both sides of the equals sign

1. $2x + 6x - 9 + 3 = 6x + 5 - 3x + 9$

2. $5x + 3x - 6 + 10 = 4x + 16 - 2x + 12$

3. $8x - 2x - 3 + 5 = 3x + 8 + 2x - 4$

4. $6x - 3x + 3 - 12 = 2x - 2 - 6x + 7$

5. $12x + 2x + 8 - 5 = 3x + 3 + 2x + 9$

6. $7x - 5x - 2 - 9 = 10x - 14 - 3x - 2$

7. $4x + x + 7 + 2 = 8x - 11 + 6x + 2$

8. $9x + 10x + 3 - 6 = 7x + 16 - 4x - 3$

9. $3x + 4x - 12 + 5 = 5x - 1 - 5x + 8$

10. $10x - 7x + 5 - 14 = 4x - 4 - 3x + 11$

CHAPTER 15   Equations with brackets

1. $6 + 3(2x + 3) = 21$

2. $2 + 5(6x - 9) = 17$

3. $6 - 8(3x - 6) = 6$

4. $10 - 4(x + 1) = 2$

5. $5 + 2(5x + 2) = 19$

6. $8 + 6(4x - 4) = 8$

7. $3 - 7(2x - 5) = 10$

8. $4 + 2(8x + 1) = 22$

9. $7 + 8(7x - 12) = 23$

10. $9 - 3(9x - 15) = 27$

CHAPTER 16   Equations with more brackets

1. $5(3x - 2) + 2(6x + 3) = 4(5x + 6)$

2. $4(5x + 7) + 7(8x - 2) = 5(8x + 10)$

3. $6(4x - 5) + 3(5x - 8) = 8(3x - 3)$

4. $5(2x - 3) - 4(4x - 6) = 3(2x - 5)$

5. $2(6x + 2) + 8(3x - 5) = 6(4x + 2)$

6. $7(9x + 4) - 5(2x + 1) = 9(6x - 4)$

7. $3(8x - 2) + 6(x + 4) = 4(7x + 10)$

8. $8(7x + 4) - 9(3x + 7) = 3(5x - 1)$

9. $9(4x - 2) + 4(7x - 3) = 2(x + 16)$

10. $12(3x + 5) + 3(9x + 1) = 7(8x + 10)$

CHAPTER 17   Substitution

1. Find the value of $4a + 2$ where $a = 4$

2. Find the value of $9x + x^2$ where $x = 3$

3. Find the value of $2y^3 + 4$ where $y = 2$

4. Find the value of $5t^2 + 4$ where $t = 6$

5. Find the value of $3n^2 - 2n$ where $n = 2$

6. Find the value of $6 - p$ where $p = -2$

7. Find the value of $3b^3 + 2b$ where $b = 2$

8. Find the value of $2z^3 - 2z$ where $z = 3$

9. Find the value of $200 - 2d^2$ where $d = 5$

10. Find the value of $8m - m^2$ where $m = 4$

CHAPTER 18   Indices

1.   Simplify $m^6 \times m^7$

2.   Simplify $a^5 \div a^3$

3.   Simplify $(2b^3)^4$

4.   Simplify y^0

5.   Simplify $4x^4 2y^3 \times 3x^2 2y$

6.   Simplify $\dfrac{45p^3q^2}{5p^2q}$

7.   Simplify $12t^5 \div 3t^2$

8.   Simplify $2w^3 x^2 \times 3w^4 x$

9.   Simplify $15y^6 \div 3y^2$

10.   Simplify $(p^3)^3$

CHAPTER 19   Factorising – Single Brackets

1. Factorise $5x - 10$

2. Factorise $6y^2 + 12y$

3. Factorise $x^2 + 7x$

4. Factorise $10x^2 - 15xy$

5. Factorise $8x - 20$

6. Factorise $8y^2 - 24xy$

7. Factorise $2y^2 - 4y$

8. Factorise $x^2 - 6x$

9. Factorise $y^2 + y$

10. Factorise $4x - 16$

CHAPTERS 20   Quadratic Equations – Expanding Brackets

1. Expand and simplify $(y + 5)(y + 7)$

2. Expand and simplify $(x + 3)(x - 4)$

3. Expand and simplify $(p + 7)(p - 8)$

4. Expand and simplify $(w + 9)(w - 4)$

5. Expand and simplify $(a - 2)(a - 3)$

6. Expand and simplify $(m - 6)(m + 5)$

7. Expand and simplify $(d + 6)(d - 2)$

8. Expand and simplify $(z + 8)(z - 3)$

9. Expand and simplify $(b + 4)(b + 6)$

10. Expand and simplify $(q + 9)(q - 4)$

CHAPTER 21   Quadratic Equations – Expanding Brackets

1. Expand and simplify $(2x + 1)(x - 4)$

2. Expand and simplify $(3d + 3)(4d - 1)$

3. Expand and simplify $(5b + 20)(b + 1)$

4. Expand and simplify $(3y + 4)(2y - 1)$

5. Expand and simplify $(3a + 5)(4a - 1)$

6. Expand and simplify $(4p - 2)(2p + 6)$

7. Expand and simplify $(6m + 3)(3m + 2)$

8. Expand and simplify $(2d - 1)(5d + 5)$

9. Expand and simplify $(8w + 2)(6w - 3)$

10. Expand and simplify $(9k + 6)(7k + 8)$

CHAPTER 22   Quadratic Equations – Expanding Brackets

1.   Expand and simplify $(x + 5)^2$

2.   Expand and simplify $(b + 7)^2$

3.   Expand and simplify $(2a + 3)^2$

4.   Expand and simplify $(3d + 6)^2$

5.   Expand and simplify $(4w - 2)^2$

6.   Expand and simplify $(y - 10)^2$

7.   Expand and simplify $(5m - 1)^2$

8.   Expand and simplify $(x + 2)^2$

9.   Expand and simplify $(6p + 4)^2$

10.   Expand and simplify $(z - 3)^2$

CHAPTER 23   Quadratic Equations – Expanding Brackets

1.   Expand and simplify $3(4x + 2)(x + 3)$

2.   Expand and simplify $2(5x + 1)(2x + 4)$

3.   Expand and simplify $4(2x + 3)(3x + 1)$

4.   Expand and simplify $7(x + 4)(4x + 3)$

5.   Expand and simplify $5(3x + 1)(x - 1)$

6.   Expand and simplify $6(7x + 2)(2x - 3)$

7.   Expand and simplify $8(9x + 5)(4x - 6)$

8.   Expand and simplify $10(6x + 6)(3x - 2)$

9.   Expand and simplify $4(3x - 2)(2x - 5)$

10.   Expand and simplify $2(5x - 1)(3x + 4)$

CHAPTER 24   Addition of two sets of double brackets

1.   Expand and simplify $(x + 7) (x - 5) + (x - 2) (x - 4)$

2.   Expand and simplify $(x + 9) (x - 1) + (x + 3) (x - 2)$

3.   Expand and simplify $(x + 2) (x + 3) + (x + 1) (x - 5)$

4.   Expand and simplify $(x + 3) (x + 4) + (x + 2) (x - 3)$

5.   Expand and simplify $(x - 2) (x + 6) + (x - 1) (x - 4)$

6.   Expand and simplify $(x + 5) (x - 2) + (x + 4) (x + 1)$

7.   Expand and simplify $(x + 4) (x + 7) + (x - 5) (x - 2)$

8.   Expand and simplify $(x + 6) (x - 3) + (x - 7) (x + 2)$

9.   Expand and simplify $(x + 8) (x - 4) + (x - 6) (x - 1)$

10.   Expand and simplify $(x - 1) (x + 9) + (x - 3) (x + 6)$

CHAPTER 25   Subtraction of two sets of double brackets

1.   Expand and simplify $(x + 7) (x + 4) - (x + 3) (x - 1)$

2.   Expand and simplify $(x + 5) (x + 6) - (x + 2) (x + 4)$

3.   Expand and simplify $(x + 3) (x - 2) - (x - 1) (x + 1)$

4.   Expand and simplify $(x + 8) (x - 1) - (x + 4) (x - 2)$

5.   Expand and simplify $(x + 6) (x - 3) - (x + 7) (x - 3)$

6.   Expand and simplify $(x - 2) (x + 7) - (x - 5) (x + 6)$

7.   Expand and simplify $(x - 4) (x - 5) - (x - 6) (x - 4)$

8.   Expand and simplify $(x + 1) (x - 8) - (x - 9) (x + 5)$

9.   Expand and simplify $(x - 9) (x + 3) - (x + 1) (x - 8)$

10.   Expand and simplify $(x - 6) (x + 9) - (x + 5) (x - 7)$

CHAPTER 26   Factorising Quadratics

1.   Factorise $x^2 + 5x + 6$

2.   Factorise $x^2 + 7x + 10$

3.   Factorise $y^2 + 7y + 12$

4.   Factorise $m^2 + 8m + 15$

5.   Factorise $x^2 + 11x + 24$

6.   Factorise $x^2 + 11x + 18$

7.   Factorise $p^2 + 9p + 18$

8.   Factorise $y^2 + 12y + 35$

9.   Factorise $m^2 + 11m + 28$

10. Factorise $x^2 + 17x + 60$

CHAPTER 27   Factorising Quadratics

1.   Factorise $x^2 - 7x + 10$

2.   Factorise $y^2 - 10y + 16$

3.   Factorise $x^2 - 3x - 10$

4.   Factorise $x^2 - 11x + 18$

5.   Factorise $p^2 - 6p + 8$

6.   Factorise $m^2 - 6m + 5$

7.   Factorise $d^2 - 9d + 20$

8.   Factorise $y^2 - 9y + 20$

9.   Factorise $z^2 - 8z + 15$

10. Factorise $x^2 - 13x + 42$

CHAPTER 28   Factorising Quadratics

1. Factorise $x^2 - 64$

2. Factorise $x^2 - 100$

3. Factorise $y^2 - 169$

4. Factorise $x^2 - 25$

5. Factorise $x^2 - 9$

6. Factorise $p^2 - 36$

7. Factorise $x^2 - 49$

8. Factorise $x^2 - 144$

9. Factorise $x^2 - 81$

10. Factorise $y^2 - 400$

CHAPTER 30   Algebraic Fractions – Simplify

1. Simplify $\dfrac{3x+6}{3}$

2. Simplify $\dfrac{12}{2x+8}$

3. Simplify $\dfrac{3x+6}{6x+12}$

4. Simplify $\dfrac{10a+8b}{2}$

5. Simplify $\dfrac{2x+10}{x^2+5x}$

6. Simplify $\dfrac{x^2+3x}{6x^2}$

7. Simplify $\dfrac{3(x+4)}{x^2+5x+4}$

8. Simplify $\dfrac{x^2-2x+1}{x^2+2x+3}$

9. Simplify $\dfrac{x-1}{x^2-3x+2}$

10. Simplify $\dfrac{2x+4}{x^2+4x+4}$

CHAPTER 32   Algebraic Fractions – Addition

1.   Simplify $\dfrac{5}{8x} + \dfrac{7}{12x}$

2.   Simplify $\dfrac{2}{x} + \dfrac{3}{4x}$

3.   Simplify $\dfrac{1}{4x} + \dfrac{1}{5x}$

4.   Simplify $\dfrac{8}{5x} + \dfrac{4}{15x}$

5.   Simplify $\dfrac{1}{3x} + \dfrac{3}{4x}$

6.   Simplify $\dfrac{5}{2x} + \dfrac{1}{3x}$

7.   Simplify $\dfrac{1}{6x} + \dfrac{3}{8x}$

8.   Simplify $\dfrac{2}{7x} + \dfrac{3}{4x}$

9.   Simplify $\dfrac{3}{8x} + \dfrac{2}{9x}$

10. Simplify $\dfrac{2}{5x} + \dfrac{3}{6x}$

CHAPTER 33   Algebraic Fractions – Addition More Complex

1. Simplify $\dfrac{4}{x+1} + \dfrac{3}{x+4}$

2. Simplify $\dfrac{1}{x+2} + \dfrac{2}{x+1}$

3. Simplify $\dfrac{4}{x+4} + \dfrac{5}{x-3}$

4. Simplify $\dfrac{3}{x+7} + \dfrac{6}{x-4}$

5. Simplify $\dfrac{5}{x+2} + \dfrac{4}{x+7}$

6. Simplify $\dfrac{4}{x+6} + \dfrac{1}{x+1}$

7. Simplify $\dfrac{2}{x+3} + \dfrac{3}{x+5}$

8. Simplify $\dfrac{3}{x+5} + \dfrac{4}{x-1}$

9. Simplify $\dfrac{2}{x+8} + \dfrac{3}{x-6}$

10. Simplify $\dfrac{7}{x-9} + \dfrac{3}{x+8}$

CHAPTER 34   Algebraic Fractions – Subtraction

1.   Simplify $\dfrac{5}{8x} - \dfrac{1}{4x}$

2.   Simplify $\dfrac{6}{7x} - \dfrac{2}{3x}$

3.   Simplify $\dfrac{12}{4x} - \dfrac{2}{x}$

4.   Simplify $\dfrac{4}{6x} - \dfrac{2}{7x}$

5.   Simplify $\dfrac{7}{9x} - \dfrac{5}{8x}$

6.   Simplify $\dfrac{6}{15x} - \dfrac{1}{5x}$

7.   Simplify $\dfrac{7}{12x} - \dfrac{3}{8x}$

8.   Simplify $\dfrac{5}{4x} - \dfrac{2}{3x}$

9.   Simplify $\dfrac{19}{18x} - \dfrac{5}{6x}$

10.   Simplify $\dfrac{9}{5x} - \dfrac{3}{4x}$

CHAPTER 35   Algebraic Fractions – Multiplication

1.   Simplify $\dfrac{3}{x} \times \dfrac{2}{7x}$

2.   Simplify $\dfrac{2y}{x} \times \dfrac{4}{x}$

3.   Simplify $\dfrac{2x+1}{x+3} \times \dfrac{x+3}{7x+5}$

4.   Simplify $\dfrac{y+4}{y-1} \times \dfrac{y+8}{y+4}$

5.   Simplify $\dfrac{y-5}{y+1} \times \dfrac{y+3}{y-2}$

6.   Simplify $\dfrac{2(p+2)}{p-6} \times \dfrac{3p-18}{p+1}$

7.   Simplify $\dfrac{8x^2+x}{x+7} \times \dfrac{1}{8x+1}$

8.   Simplify $\dfrac{a+b}{c+d} \times \dfrac{3c+3d}{2a+2b}$

9.   Simplify $\dfrac{x+10}{6x-36} \times \dfrac{x-6}{3x+2}$

10.   Simplify $\dfrac{9x+27}{5x-4} \times \dfrac{x+1}{12x+36}$

CHAPTER 36   Algebraic Fractions – Division

1.   Simplify $\dfrac{5}{x} \div \dfrac{5x}{3}$

2.   Simplify $\dfrac{6y}{x} \div \dfrac{x}{2}$

3.   Simplify $\dfrac{3x+2}{x+4} \div \dfrac{x+7}{x+4}$

4.   Simplify $\dfrac{y+3}{y-5} \div \dfrac{y-2}{y-5}$

5.   Simplify $\dfrac{y+6}{y-2} \div \dfrac{y-4}{y+3}$

6.   Simplify $\dfrac{3(x+1)}{x+2} \div \dfrac{x+5}{4x+8}$

7.   Simplify $\dfrac{6x^2-x}{x+9} \div \dfrac{6x-1}{3}$

8.   Simplify $\dfrac{x+y}{a+b} \div \dfrac{4x+4y}{3a+3b}$

9.   Simplify $\dfrac{x+12}{9x-18} \div \dfrac{5x+3}{x-2}$

10.   Simplify $\dfrac{5x+25}{7x-2} \div \dfrac{8x+40}{x-3}$

CHAPTER 37   Solving Algebraic Fractions

1. Solve $\dfrac{x}{2} + 4 = 16$

2. Solve $\dfrac{x}{5} + 2 = 6$

3. Solve $\dfrac{x}{8} + 3 = 9$

4. Solve $\dfrac{x}{4} + 7 = 14$

5. Solve $\dfrac{x}{3} + 6 = 11$

6. Solve $\dfrac{x}{9} + 5 = 8$

7. Solve $\dfrac{x}{6} + 9 = 15$

8. Solve $\dfrac{x}{7} + 8 = 10$

9. Solve $\dfrac{x}{12} + 1 = 6$

10. Solve $\dfrac{x}{11} + 12 = 18$

CHAPTER 37   Solving Algebraic Fractions – Continued

1. Solve $\dfrac{x}{3} - 1 = 6$

2. Solve $\dfrac{x}{4} - 7 = 1$

3. Solve $\dfrac{x}{7} - 6 = 0$

4. Solve $\dfrac{x}{9} - 3 = 7$

5. Solve $\dfrac{x}{6} - 4 = 5$

6. Solve $\dfrac{x}{5} - 5 = 4$

7. Solve $\dfrac{x}{8} - 2 = 3$

8. Solve $\dfrac{x}{12} - 8 = 1$

9. Solve $\dfrac{x}{2} - 16 = 8$

10. Solve $\dfrac{x}{10} - 9 = 2$

CHAPTER 38   Solving More Complex Algebraic Fractions

1. Solve $\dfrac{2x}{3} = \dfrac{2}{5}$

2. Solve $\dfrac{3x}{7} = \dfrac{5}{14}$

3. Solve $\dfrac{5x}{8} = \dfrac{1}{2}$

4. Solve $\dfrac{4x}{9} = \dfrac{1}{3}$

5. Solve $\dfrac{6x}{4} = \dfrac{1}{5}$

6. Solve $\dfrac{8x}{6} = \dfrac{4}{9}$

7. Solve $\dfrac{12x}{3} = \dfrac{1}{3}$

8. Solve $\dfrac{7x}{5} = \dfrac{2}{3}$

9. Solve $\dfrac{11x}{10} = \dfrac{2}{5}$

10. Solve $\dfrac{9x}{3} = \dfrac{1}{5}$

CHAPTER 39   Solving More Complex Algebraic Fractions – Continued

1. Solve $\dfrac{x}{4} = \dfrac{2}{3} + \dfrac{x}{6}$

2. Solve $\dfrac{x}{5} = \dfrac{1}{15} + \dfrac{x}{6}$

3. Solve $\dfrac{x}{3} = \dfrac{1}{4} + \dfrac{x}{12}$

4. Solve $\dfrac{x}{4} = \dfrac{1}{6} + \dfrac{2x}{24}$

5. Solve $\dfrac{x}{8} = \dfrac{3}{4} - \dfrac{x}{16}$

6. Solve $\dfrac{x}{9} = \dfrac{5}{6} - \dfrac{x}{18}$

7. Solve $\dfrac{x}{2} = \dfrac{3}{5} - \dfrac{x}{10}$

8. Solve $\dfrac{2x}{7} = \dfrac{8}{14} + \dfrac{3x}{21}$

9. Solve $\dfrac{3x}{18} = \dfrac{2}{3} + \dfrac{x}{9}$

10. Solve $\dfrac{5x}{6} = \dfrac{7}{8} - \dfrac{x}{24}$

CHAPTER 40   Solving More Complex Algebraic Fractions – Continued

1. Solve $\dfrac{x+4}{3} = \dfrac{3x+5}{2}$

2. Solve $\dfrac{4x+3}{8} = \dfrac{x+2}{5}$

3. Solve $\dfrac{x-6}{3} = \dfrac{x+1}{4}$

4. Solve $\dfrac{x-9}{4} = \dfrac{x-4}{6}$

5. Solve $\dfrac{8x+2}{5} = \dfrac{3x+2}{3}$

6. Solve $\dfrac{x+5}{2} = \dfrac{x-5}{7}$

7. Solve $\dfrac{6x-4}{4} = \dfrac{5x+9}{5}$

8. Solve $\dfrac{x-8}{3} = \dfrac{x-2}{9}$

9. Solve $\dfrac{3x-1}{2} = \dfrac{2x+2}{4}$

10. Solve $\dfrac{5x-5}{4} = \dfrac{5x+5}{10}$

CHAPTER 41   Solving More Complex Algebraic Fractions – Continued

1. Solve $\dfrac{9}{x-5} = \dfrac{6}{x+7}$

2. Solve $\dfrac{6}{x-3} = \dfrac{3}{x-5}$

3. Solve $\dfrac{7}{x+4} = \dfrac{2}{x-8}$

4. Solve $\dfrac{8}{x+2} = \dfrac{4}{x+4}$

5. Solve $\dfrac{3}{2x-3} = \dfrac{6}{5x+2}$

6. Solve $\dfrac{5}{6x-7} = \dfrac{10}{8x+5}$

7. Solve $\dfrac{4}{4x+3} = \dfrac{1}{6x-2}$

8. Solve $\dfrac{9}{7x-4} = \dfrac{5}{3x+4}$

9. Solve $\dfrac{10}{5x-1} = \dfrac{7}{2x+3}$

10. Solve $\dfrac{6}{8x+3} = \dfrac{2}{7x-1}$

CHAPTER 42   Solving More Complex Algebraic Fractions – Continued

1. Solve $\dfrac{5x}{x+1} - \dfrac{2}{x+3} = 5$

2. Solve $\dfrac{3x}{x+5} - \dfrac{1}{x+2} = 3$

3. Solve $\dfrac{6x}{x-2} + \dfrac{3}{x-4} = 6$

4. Solve $\dfrac{9x}{x-3} + \dfrac{5}{x+1} = 9$

5. Solve $\dfrac{2x}{2x+6} - \dfrac{7}{3x+2} = 1$

6. Solve $\dfrac{3x}{3x-4} - \dfrac{6}{5x+7} = 1$

7. Solve $\dfrac{5x}{x+2} + \dfrac{4}{2x-3} = 5$

8. Solve $\dfrac{7}{5x+1} + \dfrac{6x}{3x-4} = 2$

9. Solve $\dfrac{4}{4x+3} + \dfrac{18x}{6x-2} = 3$

10. Solve $\dfrac{6}{7x+1} + \dfrac{8x}{4x-5} = 2$

CHAPTER 43   Simultaneous Equations – Elimination Subtraction

1.   Solve $4x + 2y = 2$

$2x + 2y = 0$

2.   Solve $5x + 3y = 18$

$5x + y = 16$

3.   Solve $3x + y = 18$

$2x + y = 13$

4.   Solve $2x + 2y = 10$

$x + 2y = 6$

5.   Solve $4x + y = 14$

$x + y = 5$

6.   Solve $5x + y = 14$

$3x + y = 10$

7.   Solve $x + 3y = 7$

$x + 2y = 6$

8.   Solve $x + 9y = 13$

$x + 3y = 7$

9.   Solve $x + 5y = 15$

$x + y = 7$

10. Solve $4x + y = 23$

$3x + y = 18$

CHAPTER 44   Simultaneous Equations – Elimination Addition

1.   Solve $2x + y = 2$

           $x - 2y = 6$

2.   Solve $5x + y = 28$

           $x - y = 2$

3.   Solve $x + y = 21$

           $x - y = 7$

4.   Solve $2x + 11y = 34$

           $-2x + 14y = 16$

5.   Solve $4x + 16y = 24$

           $-4x + 9y = 1$

6.   Solve $2x + 10y = 32$

           $-2x + 3y = 7$

7.   Solve $4x + 2y = 22$

           $3x - 2y = 6$

8.   Solve $6x + 2y = 26$

           $5x - 2y = 7$

9.   Solve $2x + y = 13$

           $6x - y = 3$

10.   Solve $3x + 2y = 16$

           $2x - 2y = 4$

CHAPTER 45   Simultaneous Equations – More Complex Elimination

1.   Solve $2x + y = 10$

$3x + 4y = 20$

2.   Solve $x + 3y = 15$

$3x + 2y = 17$

3.   Solve $4x + y = 11$

$5x + 2y = 16$

4.   Solve $2x + y = 9$

$3x + 2y = 16$

5.   Solve $x + y = 10$

$4x + y = 19$

6.   Solve $3x + y = 11$

$5x + 4y = 23$

7.   Solve $x + 3y = 9$

$2x + 5y = 16$

8.   Solve $x + 5y = 19$

$3x + 4y = 24$

9.   Solve $x + 2y = 7$

$5x + 3y = 14$

10.   Solve $x + 6y = 33$

$2x + 5y = 31$

CHAPTER 46   Simultaneous Equations – More Complex Elimination

1.   Solve $2x - y = 3$
                 $3x + 4y = 10$

2.   Solve $2x - y = 4$
                 $3x + 2y = 13$

3.   Solve $2x + y = 7$
                 $6x + 5y = 23$

4.   Solve $3x - y = 9$
                 $2x + 3y = 28$

5.   Solve $3x + 4y = 25$
                 $x + 2y = 11$

6.   Solve $3x - y = 3$
                 $4x + 3y = 17$

7.   Solve $8x - y = 15$
                 $3x + 4y = 10$

8.   Solve $5x + 2y = 12$
                 $3x - 4y = 2$

9.   Solve $3x + 2y = 12$
                 $12x - 4y = 12$

10.   Solve $2x + y = 20$
                 $6x - 5y = 12$

CHAPTER 3   Subtracting a number from both sides of the equation

1. $x + 1 = 6$ $x = 5$

2. $x + 6 = 8$ $x = 2$

3. $x + 4 = 10$ $x = 6$

4. $y + 3 = 9$ $y = 6$

5. $y + 5 = 15$ $y = 10$

6. $n + 7 = 14$ $n = 7$

7. $q + 9 = 13$ $q = 4$

8. $a + 8 = 9$ $a = 1$

9. $b + 2 = 5$ $b = 3$

10. $z + 11 = 21$ $z = 10$

CHAPTER 4   Subtracting a number to both sides of the equation

1. $x - 7 = 5$ $x = 12$

2. $x - 2 = 4$ $x = 6$

3. $x - 9 = 1$ $x = 10$

4. $y - 1 = 6$ $y = 7$

5. $y - 8 = 12$ $y = 20$

6. $n - 4 = 2$ $n = 6$

7. $q - 5 = 3$ $q = 8$

8. $a - 3 = 9$ $a = 12$

9. $b - 6 = 7$ $b = 13$

10. $z - 13 = 8$ $z = 21$

CHAPTER 5   Dividing both side of the equation by the same number

1. $4x = 16$ $x = 4$

2. $8x = 56$ $x = 7$

3. $5x = 45$ $x = 9$

4. $6x = 66$ $x = 11$

5. $3x = 21$ $x = 7$

6. $7x = 56$ $x = 8$

7. $2x = 24$ $x = 12$

8. $9x = 81$ $x = 9$

9. $12x = 144$ $x = 12$

10. $15x = 90$ $x = 6$

CHAPTER 6   Multiplying both sides of the equation by the same number

1. $\dfrac{x}{2} = 16$ $x = 32$

2. $\dfrac{x}{3} = 8$ $x = 24$

3. $\dfrac{x}{6} = 9$ $x = 54$

4. $\dfrac{x}{8} = 4$ $x = 32$

5. $\dfrac{x}{7} = 12$ $x = 84$

6. $\dfrac{x}{4} = 6$ $x = 24$

7. $\dfrac{x}{9} = 11$ $x = 99$

8. $\dfrac{x}{8} = 9$ $x = 72$

9. $\dfrac{x}{12} = 8$ $x = 96$

10. $\dfrac{x}{5} = 7$ $x = 35$

CHAPTER 7   Combining Calculations – Chapter 3 and Chapter 5

1.	$4x + 7 = 27$	$x = 5$
2.	$2x + 8 = 16$	$x = 4$
3.	$6x + 4 = 40$	$x = 6$
4.	$5x + 6 = 51$	$x = 9$
5.	$9x + 5 = 68$	$x = 7$
6.	$3x + 9 = 36$	$x = 9$
7.	$7x + 5 = 33$	$x = 4$
8.	$12x + 3 = 111$	$x = 9$
9.	$8x + 11 = 99$	$x = 11$
10.	$15x + 12 = 72$	$x = 4$

CHAPTER 8   Combining Calculations – Chapter 4 and Chapter 5

1.	$4x - 4 = 12$	$x = 4$
2.	$2x - 5 = 55$	$x = 30$
3.	$7x - 3 = 32$	$x = 5$
4.	$2x - 22 = 22$	$x = 22$
5.	$8x - 6 = 66$	$x = 9$
6.	$5x - 8 = 47$	$x = 11$
7.	$9x - 7 = 101$	$x = 12$
8.	$6x - 5 = 43$	$x = 8$
9.	$3x - 4 = 71$	$x = 25$
10.	$12x - 9 = 135$	$x = 12$

CHAPTER 9   When x is a minus in the equation

1. $5 - x = 1$ $x = 4$

2. $9 - x = 6$ $x = 3$

3. $10 - x = 8$ $x = 2$

4. $8 - x = 5$ $x = 3$

5. $4 - x = 3$ $x = 1$

6. $6 - x = 2$ $x = 4$

7. $3 - x = 1$ $x = 2$

8. $7 - x = 4$ $x = 3$

9. $12 - x = 7$ $x = 5$

10. $15 - x = 9$ $x = 6$

CHAPTER 10   More complex equations − x's on both sides of the equals sign

1. $6x + 3 = 3x + 9$ $x = 2$

2. $2x + 5 = x + 10$ $x = 5$

3. $9x + 2 = 2x + 44$ $x = 6$

4. $5x + 4 = x + 48$ $x = 11$

5. $8x + 6 = 5x + 18$ $x = 4$

6. $4x + 7 = 2x + 55$ $x = 24$

7. $12x + 9 = 6x + 81$ $x = 12$

8. $7x + 8 = 4x + 35$ $x = 9$

9. $15x + 12 = 7x + 76$ $x = 8$

10. $3x + 11 = x + 37$ $x = 13$

CHAPTER 11   More complex equations – x's on both sides of the equals sign

1.	$4x - 7 = 3x - 4$	$x = 3$
2.	$6x - 6 = 2x - 2$	$x = 1$
3.	$9x - 13 = 7x - 5$	$x = 4$
4.	$5x - 27 = 2x - 6$	$x = 7$
5.	$7x - 16 = 5x - 8$	$x = 4$
6.	$8x - 38 = 3x - 8$	$x = 6$
7.	$13x - 117 = x - 9$	$x = 9$
8.	$10x - 87 = 3x - 3$	$x = 12$
9.	$12x - 89 = 3x - 8$	$x = 9$
10.	$15x - 72 = 4x - 6$	$x = 6$

CHAPTER 12   More complex equations – x's on both sides of the equals sign

1.	$4x - 5 = 3x + 8$	$x = 13$
2.	$5x - 1 = 2x + 11$	$x = 4$
3.	$9x - 32 = 2x + 3$	$x = 5$
4.	$2x - 9 = x + 7$	$x = 16$
5.	$8x - 5 = 4x + 43$	$x = 12$
6.	$7x - 15 = 2x + 40$	$x = 11$
7.	$6x - 8 = 3x + 19$	$x = 9$
8.	$17x - 9 = 2x + 51$	$x = 4$
9.	$14x - 7 = 5x + 101$	$x = 12$
10.	$15x - 4 = 3x + 68$	$x = 6$

CHAPTER 13   More complex equations – x's on both sides of the equals sign

1.	$9x - 2x = 3x + 8$	$x = 2$
2.	$8x - 3x = x + 12$	$x = 3$
3.	$12x - x = 2x + 63$	$x = 7$
4.	$11x - 4x = 3x + 24$	$x = 6$
5.	$5x - x = x + 9$	$x = 3$
6.	$6x + 4x = x + 72$	$x = 8$
7.	$7x + 8x = 3x + 144$	$x = 12$
8.	$3x + 14x = 2x + 75$	$x = 5$
9.	$2x + 22x = 16x + 56$	$x = 7$
10.	$4x + 9x = 2x + 132$	$x = 12$

CHAPTER 14   Even more complex equations x's on both sides of the equals sign

1.	$2x + 6x - 9 + 3 = 6x + 5 - 3x + 9$	$x = 4$
2.	$5x + 3x - 6 + 10 = 4x + 16 - 2x + 12$	$x = 4$
3.	$8x - 2x - 3 + 5 = 3x + 8 + 2x - 4$	$x = 2$
4.	$6x - 3x + 3 - 12 = 2x - 2 - 6x + 7$	$x = 2$
5.	$12x + 2x + 8 - 5 = 3x + 3 + 2x + 9$	$x = 1$
6.	$7x - 5x - 2 - 9 = 10x - 14 - 3x - 2$	$x = 1$
7.	$4x + x + 7 + 2 = 8x - 11 + 6x + 2$	$x = 2$
8.	$9x + 10x + 3 - 6 = 7x + 16 - 4x - 3$	$x = 1$
9.	$3x + 4x - 12 + 5 = 5x - 1 - 5x + 8$	$x = 2$
10.	$10x - 7x + 5 - 14 = 4x - 4 - 3x + 11$	$x = 8$

CHAPTER 15   Equations with brackets

1.	$6 + 3(2x + 3) = 21$	$x = 1$
2.	$2 + 5(6x - 9) = 17$	$x = 2$
3.	$6 - 8(3x - 6) = 6$	$x = 2$
4.	$10 - 4(x + 1) = 2$	$x = 1$
5.	$5 + 2(5x + 2) = 19$	$x = 1$
6.	$8 + 6(4x - 4) = 8$	$x = 1$
7.	$3 - 7(2x - 5) = 10$	$x = 2$
8.	$4 + 2(8x + 1) = 22$	$x = 1$
9.	$7 + 8(7x - 12) = 23$	$x = 2$
10.	$9 - 3(9x - 15) = 27$	$x = 1$

CHAPTER 16   Equations with more brackets

1.	$5(3x - 2) + 2(6x + 3) = 4(5x + 6)$	$x = 4$
2.	$4(5x + 7) + 7(8x - 2) = 5(8x + 10)$	$x = 1$
3.	$6(4x - 5) + 3(5x - 8) = 8(3x - 3)$	$x = 2$
4.	$5(2x - 3) - 4(4x - 6) = 3(2x - 5)$	$x = 2$
5.	$2(6x + 2) + 8(3x - 5) = 6(4x + 2)$	$x = 4$
6.	$7(9x + 4) - 5(2x + 1) = 9(6x - 4)$	$x = 59$
7.	$3(8x - 2) + 6(x + 4) = 4(7x + 10)$	$x = 11$
8.	$8(7x + 4) - 9(3x + 7) = 3(5x - 1)$	$x = 2$
9.	$9(4x - 2) + 4(7x - 3) = 2(x + 16)$	$x = 1$
10.	$12(3x + 5) + 3(9x + 1) = 7(8x + 10)$	$x = 1$

CHAPTER 17   Substitution

1. Find the value of $4a + 2$ where $a = 4$ Ans = 18

2. Find the value of $9x + x^2$ where $x = 3$ Ans = 36

3. Find the value of $2y^3 + 4$ where $y = 2$ Ans = 20

4. Find the value of $5t^2 + 4$ where $t = 6$ Ans = 184

5. Find the value of $3n^2 - 2n$ where $n = 2$ Ans = 8

6. Find the value of $6 - p$ where $p = -2$ Ans = 8

7. Find the value of $3b^3 + 2b$ where $b = 2$ Ans = 28

8. Find the value of $2z^3 - 2z$ where $z = 3$ Ans = 48

9. Find the value of $200 - 2d^2$ where $d = 5$ Ans = 150

10. Find the value of $8m - m^2$ where $m = 4$ Ans = 16

CHAPTER 18   Indices

1. Simplify $m^6 \times m^7$ $=$ m^{13}

2. Simplify $a^5 \div a^3$ $=$ a^2

3. Simplify $(2b^3)^4$ $=$ $16b^{12}$

4. Simplify y^0 $=$ 1

5. Simplify $4x^4\,2y^3 \times 3x^2\,2y$ $=$ $12x^6\,4y^4$

6. Simplify $\dfrac{45p^3q^2}{5p^2q}$ $=$ $9pq$

7. Simplify $12t^5 \div 3t^2$ $=$ $4t^3$

8. Simplify $2w^3x^2 \times 3w^4x$ $=$ $6w^7x^3$

9. Simplify $15y^6 \div 3y^2$ $=$ $5y^4$

10. Simplify $(p^3)^3$ $=$ p^9

CHAPTER 19   Factorising – Single Brackets

1. Factorise $5x - 10$ = $5(x - 2)$

2. Factorise $6y^2 + 12y$ = $6y(y + 2)$

3. Factorise $x^2 + 7x$ = $x(x + 7)$

4. Factorise $10x^2 - 15xy$ = $5x(2x - 3y)$

5. Factorise $8x - 20$ = $4(2x - 5)$

6. Factorise $8y^2 - 24xy$ = $8y(y - 3x)$

7. Factorise $2y^2 - 4y$ = $2y(y - 2)$

8. Factorise $x^2 - 6x$ = $x(x - 6)$

9. Factorise $y^2 + y$ = $y(y + 1)$

10. Factorise $4x - 16$ = $4(x - 4)$

CHAPTER 20   Quadratic Equations – Expanding Brackets

1.   Expand and simplify $(y + 5)(y + 7)$ = $y^2 + 12y + 35$
2.   Expand and simplify $(x + 3)(x - 4)$ = $x^2 - x - 12$
3.   Expand and simplify $(p + 7)(p - 8)$ = $p^2 - p - 56$
4.   Expand and simplify $(w + 9)(w - 4)$ = $w^2 + 5w - 36$
5.   Expand and simplify $(a - 2)(a - 3)$ = $a^2 - 5a + 6$
6.   Expand and simplify $(m - 6)(m + 5)$ = $m^2 - m - 30$
7.   Expand and simplify $(d + 6)(d - 2)$ = $d^2 + 4d - 12$
8.   Expand and simplify $(z + 8)(z - 3)$ = $z^2 + 5z - 24$
9.   Expand and simplify $(b + 4)(b + 6)$ = $b^2 + 10b + 24$
10. Expand and simplify $(q + 9)(q - 4)$ = $q^2 + 5q - 36$

CHAPTER 21   Quadratic Equations – Expanding Brackets

1.   Expand and simplify $(2x + 1)(x - 4)$ = $2x^2 - 7x - 4$
2.   Expand and simplify $(3d + 3)(4d - 1)$ = $12d^2 + 9d - 3$
3.   Expand and simplify $(5b + 20)(b + 1)$ = $5b^2 + 25b + 20$
4.   Expand and simplify $(3y + 4)(2y - 1)$ = $6y^2 + 5y - 4$
5.   Expand and simplify $(3a + 5)(4a - 1)$ = $12a^2 + 17a - 5$
6.   Expand and simplify $(4p - 2)(2p + 6)$ = $8p^2 + 20p - 12$
7.   Expand and simplify $(6m + 3)(3m + 2)$ = $18m^2 + 21m + 6$
8.   Expand and simplify $(2d - 1)(5d + 5)$ = $10d^2 + 5d - 5$
9.   Expand and simplify $(8w + 2)(6w - 3)$ = $48w^2 - 12w - 6$
10. Expand and simplify $(9k + 6)(7k + 8)$ = $63k^2 + 114k + 48$

CHAPTER 22   Quadratic Equations – Expanding Brackets

1.   Expand and simplify $(x + 5)^2$ $= x^2 + 10x + 25$

2.   Expand and simplify $(b + 7)^2$ $= b^2 + 14b + 49$

3.   Expand and simplify $(2a + 3)^2$ $= 4a^2 + 12a + 9$

4.   Expand and simplify $(3d + 6)^2$ $= 9d^2 + 36d + 36$

5.   Expand and simplify $(4w - 2)^2$ $= 16w^2 - 16w + 4$

6.   Expand and simplify $(y - 10)^2$ $= y^2 - 20y + 100$

7.   Expand and simplify $(5m -1)^2$ $= 25m^2 - 10m + 1$

8.   Expand and simplify $(x + 2)^2$ $= x^2 + 4x + 4$

9.   Expand and simplify $(6p + 4)^2$ $= 36p^2 + 48p + 16$

10.   Expand and simplify $(z - 3)^2$ $= z^2 - 6z + 9$

CHAPTER 23   Quadratic Equations – Expanding Brackets

1.   Expand and simplify $3(4x + 2)(x + 3)$ $= 12x^2 + 42x + 18$

2.   Expand and simplify $2(5x + 1)(2x + 4)$ $= 20x^2 + 44x + 8$

3.   Expand and simplify $4(2x + 3)(3x + 1)$ $= 24x^2 + 44x + 12$

4.   Expand and simplify $7(x + 4)(4x + 3)$ $= 28x^2 + 133x + 84$

5.   Expand and simplify $5(3x + 1)(x - 1)$ $= 15x^2 - 10x - 5$

6.   Expand and simplify $6(7x + 2)(2x - 3)$ $= 84x^2 - 102x - 36$

7.   Expand and simplify $8(9x + 5)(4x - 6)$ $= 288x^2 - 272x - 240$

8.   Expand and simplify $10(6x + 6)(3x - 2)$ $= 180x^2 + 60x - 120$

9.   Expand and simplify $4(3x - 2)(2x - 5)$ $= 24x^2 - 76x + 40$

10.   Expand and simplify $2(5x - 1)(3x + 4)$ $= 30x^2 + 36x - 8$

CHAPTER 24   Addition of two sets of double brackets

1.   Expand and simplify $(x + 7)(x - 5) + (x - 2)(x - 4)$ $= 2x^2 - 4x - 27$

2.   Expand and simplify $(x + 9)(x - 1) + (x + 3)(x - 2)$ $= 2x^2 + 9x - 15$

3.   Expand and simplify $(x + 2)(x + 3) + (x + 1)(x - 5)$ $= 2x^2 + x + 1$

4.   Expand and simplify $(x + 3)(x + 4) + (x + 2)(x - 3)$ $= 2x^2 + 6x + 6$

5.   Expand and simplify $(x - 2)(x + 6) + (x - 1)(x - 4)$ $= 2x^2 - x - 8$

6.   Expand and simplify $(x + 5)(x - 2) + (x + 4)(x + 1)$ $= 2x^2 + 8x - 6$

7.   Expand and simplify $(x + 4)(x + 7) + (x - 5)(x - 2)$ $= 2x^2 + 4x + 38$

8.   Expand and simplify $(x + 6)(x - 3) + (x - 7)(x + 2)$ $= 2x^2 - 2x - 32$

9.   Expand and simplify $(x + 8)(x - 4) + (x - 6)(x - 1)$ $= 2x^2 - 3x - 26$

10. Expand and simplify $(x - 1)(x + 9) + (x - 3)(x + 6)$ $= 2x^2 + 11x - 27$

CHAPTER 25   Subtraction of two sets of double brackets

1.   Expand and simplify $(x + 7)(x + 4) - (x + 3)(x - 1)$ $= 9x + 31$

2.   Expand and simplify $(x + 5)(x + 6) - (x + 2)(x + 4)$ $= 5x + 22$

3.   Expand and simplify $(x + 3)(x - 2) - (x - 1)(x + 1)$ $= x - 5$

4.   Expand and simplify $(x + 8)(x - 1) - (x + 4)(x - 2)$ $= 5x$

5.   Expand and simplify $(x + 6)(x - 3) - (x + 7)(x - 3)$ $= -x + 3$

6.   Expand and simplify $(x - 2)(x + 7) - (x - 5)(x + 6)$ $= 4x + 26$

7.   Expand and simplify $(x - 4)(x - 5) - (x - 6)(x - 4)$ $= x - 4$

8.   Expand and simplify $(x + 1)(x - 8) - (x - 9)(x + 5)$ $= -3x + 37$

9.   Expand and simplify $(x - 9)(x + 3) - (x + 1)(x - 8)$ $= x - 19$

10. Expand and simplify $(x - 6)(x + 9) - (x + 5)(x - 7)$ $= 5x - 19$

CHAPTER 26   Factorising Quadratics

1.   Factorise $x^2 + 5x + 6$ = $(x + 3)(x + 2)$
2.   Factorise $x^2 + 7x + 10$ = $(x + 2)(x + 5)$
3.   Factorise $y^2 + 7y + 12$ = $(y + 3)(y + 4)$
4.   Factorise $m^2 + 8m + 15$ = $(m + 5)(m + 3)$
5.   Factorise $x^2 + 11x + 24$ = $(x + 3)(x + 8)$
6.   Factorise $x^2 + 11x + 18$ = $(x + 9)(x + 2)$
7.   Factorise $p^2 + 9p + 18$ = $(p + 3)(p + 6)$
8.   Factorise $y^2 + 12y + 35$ = $(y + 5)(y + 7)$
9.   Factorise $m^2 + 11m + 28$ = $(m + 4)(m + 7)$
10. Factorise $x^2 + 17x + 60$ = $(x + 5)(x + 12)$

CHAPTER 27   Factorising Quadratics

1.   Factorise $x^2 - 7x + 10$ = $(x - 2)(x - 5)$
2.   Factorise $y^2 - 10y + 16$ = $(y - 2)(y - 8)$
3.   Factorise $x^2 - 3x - 10$ = $(x + 2)(x - 5)$
4.   Factorise $x^2 - 11x + 18$ = $(x - 2)(x - 9)$
5.   Factorise $p^2 - 6p + 8$ = $(p - 2)(p - 4)$
6.   Factorise $m^2 - 6m + 5$ = $(m - 1)(m - 5)$
7.   Factorise $d^2 - 9d + 20$ = $(d - 4)(d - 5)$
8.   Factorise $y^2 - 9y + 18$ = $(y - 6)(y - 3)$
9.   Factorise $z^2 - 8z + 15$ = $(z - 3)(z - 5)$
10. Factorise $x^2 - 13x + 42$ = $(x - 7)(x - 6)$

CHAPTER 28   Factorising Quadratics

1.   Factorise $x^2 - 64$ = $(x + 8)(x - 8)$

2.   Factorise $x^2 - 100$ = $(x + 10)(x - 10)$

3.   Factorise $y^2 - 169$ = $(y + 13)(y - 13)$

4.   Factorise $x^2 - 25$ = $(x + 5)(x - 5)$

5.   Factorise $x^2 - 9$ = $(x + 3)(x - 3)$

6.   Factorise $p^2 - 36$ = $(p + 6)(p - 6)$

7.   Factorise $x^2 - 49$ = $(x + 7)(x - 7)$

8.   Factorise $x^2 - 144$ = $(x + 12)(x - 12)$

9.   Factorise $x^2 - 81$ = $(x + 9)(x - 9)$

10. Factorise $y^2 - 400$ = $(y + 20)(y - 20)$

CHAPTERS 30   Algebraic Fractions – Simplify

1. Simplify $\dfrac{3x+6}{3}$ $=$ $x+2$

2. Simplify $\dfrac{12}{2x+8}$ $=$ $\dfrac{6}{x+4}$

3. Simplify $\dfrac{3x+6}{6x+12}$ $=$ $\dfrac{1}{2}$

4. Simplify $\dfrac{10a+8b}{2}$ $=$ $5a+4b$

5. Simplify $\dfrac{2x+10}{x^2+5x}$ $=$ $\dfrac{2}{x}$

6. Simplify $\dfrac{x^2+3x}{6x^2}$ $=$ $\dfrac{x+3}{6x}$

7. Simplify $\dfrac{3(x+4)}{x^2+5x+4}$ $=$ $\dfrac{3}{x+1}$

8. Simplify $\dfrac{x^2-2x+1}{x^2+2x+3}$ $=$ $\dfrac{x-1}{x+3}$

9. Simplify $\dfrac{x-1}{x^2-3x+2}$ $=$ $\dfrac{1}{x-2}$

10. Simplify $\dfrac{2x+4}{x^2+4x+4}$ $=$ $\dfrac{2}{x+2}$

CHAPTER 32   Algebraic Fractions – Addition

1. Simplify $\dfrac{5}{8x} + \dfrac{7}{12x}$ $= \dfrac{29}{24x}$

2. Simplify $\dfrac{2}{x} + \dfrac{3}{4x}$ $= \dfrac{11}{4x}$

3. Simplify $\dfrac{1}{4x} + \dfrac{1}{5x}$ $= \dfrac{9}{20x}$

4. Simplify $\dfrac{8}{5x} + \dfrac{4}{15x}$ $= \dfrac{28}{15x}$

5. Simplify $\dfrac{1}{3x} + \dfrac{3}{4x}$ $= \dfrac{13}{12x}$

6. Simplify $\dfrac{5}{2x} + \dfrac{1}{3x}$ $= \dfrac{17}{6x}$

7. Simplify $\dfrac{1}{6x} + \dfrac{3}{8x}$ $= \dfrac{13}{24x}$

8. Simplify $\dfrac{2}{7x} + \dfrac{3}{4x}$ $= \dfrac{29}{28x}$

9. Simplify $\dfrac{3}{8x} + \dfrac{2}{9x}$ $= \dfrac{43}{72x}$

10. Simplify $\dfrac{2}{5x} + \dfrac{3}{6x}$ $= \dfrac{9}{10x}$

CHAPTER 33   Algebraic Fractions – Addition More Complex

1. Simplify $\dfrac{4}{x+1} + \dfrac{3}{x+4}$ $= \dfrac{7x+19}{(x+1)(x+4)}$

2. Simplify $\dfrac{1}{x+2} + \dfrac{2}{x+1}$ $= \dfrac{3x+5}{(x+2)(x+1)}$

3. Simplify $\dfrac{4}{x+4} + \dfrac{5}{x-3}$ $= \dfrac{9x+8}{(x+4)(x-3)}$

4. Simplify $\dfrac{3}{x+7} + \dfrac{6}{x-4}$ $= \dfrac{3(3x+10)}{(x+7)(x-4)}$

5. Simplify $\dfrac{5}{x+2} + \dfrac{4}{x+7}$ $= \dfrac{9x+43}{(x+2)(x+7)}$

6. Simplify $\dfrac{4}{x+6} + \dfrac{1}{x+1}$ $= \dfrac{5(x+2)}{(x+6)(x-1)}$

7. Simplify $\dfrac{2}{x+3} + \dfrac{3}{x+5}$ $= \dfrac{5x+19}{(x+3)(x+5)}$

8. Simplify $\dfrac{3}{x+5} + \dfrac{4}{x-1}$ $= \dfrac{7x+17}{(x+5)(x-1)}$

9. Simplify $\dfrac{2}{x+8} + \dfrac{3}{x-6}$ $= \dfrac{5x+12}{(x+8)(x-6)}$

10. Simplify $\dfrac{7}{x-9} + \dfrac{3}{x+8}$ $= \dfrac{10x+29}{(x-9)(x+8)}$

CHAPTER 34   Algebraic Fractions – Subtraction

1.   Simplify $\dfrac{5}{8x} - \dfrac{1}{4x}$ $=$ $\dfrac{3}{8x}$

2.   Simplify $\dfrac{6}{7x} - \dfrac{2}{3x}$ $=$ $\dfrac{4}{21x}$

3.   Simplify $\dfrac{12}{4x} - \dfrac{2}{x}$ $=$ $\dfrac{1}{x}$

4.   Simplify $\dfrac{4}{6x} - \dfrac{2}{7x}$ $=$ $\dfrac{8}{21x}$

5.   Simplify $\dfrac{7}{9x} - \dfrac{5}{8x}$ $=$ $\dfrac{11}{72x}$

6.   Simplify $\dfrac{6}{15x} - \dfrac{1}{5x}$ $=$ $\dfrac{1}{5x}$

7.   Simplify $\dfrac{7}{12x} - \dfrac{3}{8x}$ $=$ $\dfrac{5}{24x}$

8.   Simplify $\dfrac{5}{4x} - \dfrac{2}{3x}$ $=$ $\dfrac{7}{12x}$

9.   Simplify $\dfrac{19}{18x} - \dfrac{5}{6x}$ $=$ $\dfrac{2}{9x}$

10. Simplify $\dfrac{9}{5x} - \dfrac{3}{4x}$ $=$ $\dfrac{21}{20x}$

CHAPTER 35   Algebraic Fractions – Multiplication

1.   Simplify $\dfrac{3}{x} \times \dfrac{2}{7x}$ $=$ $\dfrac{6}{7x^2}$

2.   Simplify $\dfrac{2y}{x} \times \dfrac{4}{x}$ $=$ $\dfrac{8y}{x^2}$

3.   Simplify $\dfrac{2x+1}{x+3} \times \dfrac{x+3}{7x+5}$ $=$ $\dfrac{2x+1}{7x+5}$

4.   Simplify $\dfrac{y+4}{y-1} \times \dfrac{y+8}{y+4}$ $=$ $\dfrac{y+8}{y-1}$

5.   Simplify $\dfrac{y-5}{y+1} \times \dfrac{y+3}{y-2}$ $=$ $\dfrac{(y-5)(y+3)}{(y+1)(y-2)}$

6.   Simplify $\dfrac{2(p+2)}{p-6} \times \dfrac{3p-18}{p+1}$ $=$ $\dfrac{6(p+2)}{p+1}$

7.   Simplify $\dfrac{8x^2+x}{x+7} \times \dfrac{1}{8x+1}$ $=$ $\dfrac{x}{x+7}$

8.   Simplify $\dfrac{a+b}{c+d} \times \dfrac{3c+3d}{2a+2b}$ $=$ $\dfrac{3}{2}$

9.   Simplify $\dfrac{x+10}{6x-36} \times \dfrac{x-6}{3x+2}$ $=$ $\dfrac{x+10}{6(3x+2)}$

10.   Simplify $\dfrac{9x+27}{5x-4} \times \dfrac{x+1}{12x+36}$ $=$ $\dfrac{9(x+1)}{12(5x+4)}$

CHAPTER 36   Algebraic Fractions – Division

1.   Simplify $\dfrac{5}{x} \div \dfrac{5x}{3}$ $=$ $\dfrac{3}{x^2}$

2.   Simplify $\dfrac{6y}{x} \div \dfrac{x}{2}$ $=$ $\dfrac{12y}{x^2}$

3.   Simplify $\dfrac{3x+2}{x+4} \div \dfrac{x+7}{x+4}$ $=$ $\dfrac{3x+2}{x+7}$

4.   Simplify $\dfrac{y+3}{y-5} \div \dfrac{y-2}{y-5}$ $=$ $\dfrac{y+3}{y-2}$

5.   Simplify $\dfrac{y+6}{y-2} \div \dfrac{y-4}{y+3}$ $=$ $\dfrac{(y+6)(y+3)}{(y-2)(y-4)}$

6.   Simplify $\dfrac{3(x+1)}{x+2} \div \dfrac{x+5}{4x+8}$ $=$ $\dfrac{12(x+1)}{x+5}$

7.   Simplify $\dfrac{6x^2-x}{x+9} \div \dfrac{6x-1}{3}$ $=$ $\dfrac{3x}{x+9}$

8.   Simplify $\dfrac{x+y}{a+b} \div \dfrac{4x+4y}{3a+3b}$ $=$ $\dfrac{3}{4}$

9.   Simplify $\dfrac{x+12}{9x-18} \div \dfrac{5x+3}{x-2}$ $=$ $\dfrac{x+12}{9(5x+3)}$

10.   Simplify $\dfrac{5x+25}{7x-2} \div \dfrac{8x+40}{x-3}$ $=$ $\dfrac{5(x-3)}{8(7x-2)}$

CHAPTER 37   Solving Algebraic Fractions

1. Solve $\dfrac{x}{2} + 4 = 16$ $x = 24$

2. Solve $\dfrac{x}{5} + 2 = 6$ $x = 20$

3. Solve $\dfrac{x}{8} + 3 = 9$ $x = 48$

4. Solve $\dfrac{x}{4} + 7 = 14$ $x = 28$

5. Solve $\dfrac{x}{3} + 6 = 11$ $x = 15$

6. Solve $\dfrac{x}{9} + 5 = 8$ $x = 27$

7. Solve $\dfrac{x}{6} + 9 = 15$ $x = 36$

8. Solve $\dfrac{x}{7} + 8 = 10$ $x = 14$

9. Solve $\dfrac{x}{12} + 1 = 6$ $x = 60$

10. Solve $\dfrac{x}{11} + 12 = 18$ $x = 66$

CHAPTER 37   Solving Algebraic Fractions – Continued

1. Solve $\dfrac{x}{3} - 1 = 6$ $x = 21$

2. Solve $\dfrac{x}{4} - 7 = 1$ $x = 32$

3. Solve $\dfrac{x}{7} - 6 = 0$ $x = 42$

4. Solve $\dfrac{x}{9} - 3 = 7$ $x = 90$

5. Solve $\dfrac{x}{6} - 4 = 5$ $x = 54$

6. Solve $\dfrac{x}{5} - 5 = 4$ $x = 45$

7. Solve $\dfrac{x}{8} - 2 = 3$ $x = 40$

8. Solve $\dfrac{x}{12} - 8 = 1$ $x = 108$

9. Solve $\dfrac{x}{2} - 16 = 8$ $x = 48$

10. Solve $\dfrac{x}{10} - 9 = 2$ $x = 110$

CHAPTER 38   Solving More Complex Algebraic Fractions

1. Solve $\dfrac{2x}{3} = \dfrac{2}{5}$ $x = \dfrac{3}{5}$

2. Solve $\dfrac{3x}{7} = \dfrac{5}{14}$ $x = \dfrac{5}{6}$

3. Solve $\dfrac{5x}{8} = \dfrac{1}{2}$ $x = \dfrac{4}{5}$

4. Solve $\dfrac{4x}{9} = \dfrac{1}{3}$ $x = \dfrac{3}{4}$

5. Solve $\dfrac{6x}{4} = \dfrac{1}{5}$ $x = \dfrac{2}{15}$

6. Solve $\dfrac{8x}{6} = \dfrac{4}{9}$ $x = \dfrac{1}{3}$

7. Solve $\dfrac{12x}{3} = \dfrac{1}{3}$ $x = \dfrac{1}{12}$

8. Solve $\dfrac{7x}{5} = \dfrac{2}{3}$ $x = \dfrac{10}{21}$

9. Solve $\dfrac{11x}{10} = \dfrac{2}{5}$ $x = \dfrac{4}{11}$

10. Solve $\dfrac{9x}{3} = \dfrac{1}{5}$ $x = \dfrac{1}{15}$

CHAPTER 39   Solving More Complex Algebraic Fractions – Continued

1. Solve $\dfrac{x}{4} = \dfrac{2}{3} + \dfrac{x}{6}$ $x = 8$

2. Solve $\dfrac{x}{5} = \dfrac{1}{15} + \dfrac{x}{6}$ $x = 2$

3. Solve $\dfrac{x}{3} = \dfrac{1}{4} + \dfrac{x}{12}$ $x = 1$

4. Solve $\dfrac{x}{4} = \dfrac{1}{6} + \dfrac{2x}{24}$ $x = 1$

5. Solve $\dfrac{x}{8} = \dfrac{3}{4} - \dfrac{x}{16}$ $x = 4$

6. Solve $\dfrac{x}{9} = \dfrac{5}{6} - \dfrac{x}{18}$ $x = 5$

7. Solve $\dfrac{x}{2} = \dfrac{3}{5} - \dfrac{x}{10}$ $x = 1$

8. Solve $\dfrac{2x}{7} = \dfrac{8}{14} + \dfrac{3x}{21}$ $x = 4$

9. Solve $\dfrac{3x}{18} = \dfrac{2}{3} + \dfrac{x}{9}$ $x = 12$

10. Solve $\dfrac{5x}{6} = \dfrac{7}{8} - \dfrac{x}{24}$ $x = 1$

CHAPTER 40   Solving More Complex Algebraic Fractions – Continued

1. Solve $\dfrac{x+4}{3} = \dfrac{3x+5}{2}$ $x = -1$

2. Solve $\dfrac{4x+3}{8} = \dfrac{x+2}{5}$ $x = \dfrac{1}{12}$

3. Solve $\dfrac{x-6}{3} = \dfrac{x+1}{4}$ $x = 27$

4. Solve $\dfrac{x-9}{4} = \dfrac{x-4}{6}$ $x = 19$

5. Solve $\dfrac{8x+2}{5} = \dfrac{3x+2}{3}$ $x = \dfrac{4}{9}$

6. Solve $\dfrac{x+5}{2} = \dfrac{x-5}{7}$ $x = -9$

7. Solve $\dfrac{6x-4}{4} = \dfrac{5x+9}{5}$ $x = \dfrac{28}{5}$

8. Solve $\dfrac{x-8}{3} = \dfrac{x-2}{9}$ $x = 11$

9. Solve $\dfrac{3x-1}{2} = \dfrac{2x+2}{4}$ $x = 1$

10. Solve $\dfrac{5x-5}{4} = \dfrac{5x+5}{10}$ $x = \dfrac{7}{3}$

CHAPTER 41   Solving More Complex Algebraic Fractions – Continued

1. Solve $\dfrac{9}{x-5} = \dfrac{6}{x+7}$ $x = -31$

2. Solve $\dfrac{6}{x-3} = \dfrac{3}{x-5}$ $x = 7$

3. Solve $\dfrac{7}{x+4} = \dfrac{2}{x-8}$ $x = \dfrac{64}{5}$

4. Solve $\dfrac{8}{x+2} = \dfrac{4}{x+4}$ $x = -6$

5. Solve $\dfrac{3}{2x-3} = \dfrac{6}{5x+2}$ $x = -8$

6. Solve $\dfrac{5}{6x-7} = \dfrac{10}{8x+5}$ $x = \dfrac{19}{4}$

7. Solve $\dfrac{4}{4x+3} = \dfrac{1}{6x-2}$ $x = \dfrac{11}{20}$

8. Solve $\dfrac{9}{7x-4} = \dfrac{5}{3x+4}$ $x = 7$

9. Solve $\dfrac{10}{5x-1} = \dfrac{7}{2x+3}$ $x = \dfrac{37}{15}$

10. Solve $\dfrac{6}{8x+3} = \dfrac{2}{7x-1}$ $x = \dfrac{6}{13}$

CHAPTER 42   Solving More Complex Algebraic Fractions – Continued

1. Solve $\dfrac{5x}{x+1} - \dfrac{2}{x+3} = 5$ $x = \dfrac{-17}{7}$

2. Solve $\dfrac{3x}{x+5} - \dfrac{1}{x+2} = 3$ $x = \dfrac{-35}{16}$

3. Solve $\dfrac{6x}{x-2} + \dfrac{3}{x-4} = 6$ $x = \dfrac{18}{5}$

4. Solve $\dfrac{9x}{x-3} + \dfrac{5}{x+1} = 9$ $x = \dfrac{-3}{8}$

5. Solve $\dfrac{2x}{2x+6} - \dfrac{7}{3x+2} = 1$ $x = \dfrac{-27}{16}$

6. Solve $\dfrac{3x}{3x-4} - \dfrac{6}{5x+7} = 1$ $x = $ -26

7. Solve $\dfrac{5x}{x+2} + \dfrac{4}{2x-3} = 5$ $x = \dfrac{19}{8}$

8. Solve $\dfrac{7}{5x+1} + \dfrac{6x}{3x-4} = 2$ $x = \dfrac{20}{61}$

9. Solve $\dfrac{4}{4x+3} + \dfrac{18x}{6x-2} = 3$ $x = \dfrac{-10}{48}$

10. Solve $\dfrac{6}{7x+1} + \dfrac{8x}{4x-5} = 2$ $x = \dfrac{10}{47}$

CHAPTER 43   Simultaneous Equations – Elimination Subtraction

1.   Solve $4x + 2y = 2$ $x = 1$
                $2x + 2y = 0$ $y = -1$

2.   Solve $5x + 3y = 18$ $x = 3$
                $5x + y = 16$ $y = 1$

3.   Solve $3x + y = 18$ $x = 5$
                $2x + y = 13$ $y = 3$

4.   Solve $2x + 2y = 10$ $x = 4$
                $x + 2y = 6$ $y = 1$

5.   Solve $4x + y = 14$ $x = 3$
                $x + y = 5$ $y = 2$

6.   Solve $5x + y = 14$ $x = 2$
                $3x + y = 10$ $y = 4$

7.   Solve $x + 3y = 7$ $x = 4$
                $x + 2y = 6$ $y = 1$

8.   Solve $x + 9y = 13$ $x = 4$
                $x + 3y = 7$ $y = 1$

9.   Solve $x + 5y = 15$ $x = 5$
                $x + y = 7$ $y = 2$

10. Solve $4x + y = 23$ $x = 5$
                $3x + y = 18$ $y = 3$

CHAPTER 44   Simultaneous Equations – Elimination Addition

1.   Solve $2x + y = 2$ $x = 2$
                    $x - 2y = 6$ $y = -2$

2.   Solve $5x + y = 28$ $x = 5$
                    $x - y = 2$ $y = 3$

3.   Solve $x + y = 21$ $x = 14$
                    $x - y = 7$ $y = 7$

4.   Solve $2x + 11y = 34$ $x = 6$
                    $-2x + 14y = 16$ $y = 2$

5.   Solve $4x + 16y = 24$ $x = 2$
                    $-4x + 9y = 1$ $y = 1$

6.   Solve $2x + 10y = 32$ $x = 1$
                    $-2x + 3y = 7$ $y = 3$

7.   Solve $4x + 2y = 22$ $x = 4$
                    $3x - 2y = 6$ $y = 3$

8.   Solve $6x + 2y = 26$ $x = 3$
                    $5x - 2y = 7$ $y = 4$

9.   Solve $2x + y = 13$ $x = 2$
                    $6x - y = 3$ $y = 9$

10.   Solve $3x + 2y = 16$ $x = 4$
                    $2x - 2y = 4$ $y = 2$

CHAPTER 45   Simultaneous Equations – More Complex Elimination

1.   Solve $2x + y = 10$ $x = 4$

$3x + 4y = 20$ $y = 2$

2.   Solve $x + 3y = 15$ $x = 3$

$3x + 2y = 17$ $y = 4$

3.   Solve $4x + y = 11$ $x = 2$

$5x + 2y = 16$ $y = 3$

4.   Solve $2x + y = 9$ $x = 2$

$3x + 2y = 16$ $y = 5$

5.   Solve $x + y = 10$ $x = 3$

$4x + y = 19$ $y = 7$

6.   Solve $3x + y = 11$ $x = 3$

$5x + 4y = 23$ $y = 2$

7.   Solve $x + 3y = 9$ $x = 3$

$2x + 5y = 16$ $y = 2$

8.   Solve $x + 5y = 19$ $x = 4$

$3x + 4y = 24$ $y = 3$

9.   Solve $x + 2y = 7$ $x = 1$

$5x + 3y = 14$ $y = 3$

10.   Solve $x + 6y = 33$ $x = 3$

$2x + 5y = 31$ $y = 5$

CHAPTER 46   Simultaneous Equations – More Complex Elimination

1.   Solve $2x - y = 3$ $x = 2$
                $3x + 4y = 10$ $y = 1$

2.   Solve $2x - y = 4$ $x = 3$
                $3x + 2y = 13$ $y = 2$

3.   Solve $2x + y = 7$ $x = 3$
                $6x + 5y = 23$ $y = 1$

4.   Solve $3x - y = 9$ $x = 5$
                $2x + 3y = 28$ $y = 6$

5.   Solve $3x + 4y = 25$ $x = 3$
                $x + 2y = 11$ $y = 4$

6.   Solve $3x - y = 3$ $x = 2$
                $4x + 3y = 17$ $y = 3$

7.   Solve $8x - y = 15$ $x = 2$
                $3x + 4y = 10$ $y = 1$

8.   Solve $5x + 2y = 12$ $x = 2$
                $3x - 4y = 2$ $y = 1$

9.   Solve $3x + 2y = 12$ $x = 2$
                $12x - 4y = 12$ $y = 3$

10.   Solve $2x + y = 20$ $x = 7$
                $6x - 5y = 12$ $y = 6$

Made in the USA
Monee, IL
24 August 2021